# TEACHER'S PET PUBLICATIONS

LITPLAN TEACHER PACK™
for
The Outsiders
based on the book by
S. E. Hinton

Written by
Mary B. Collins

ISBN 978-1-60249-228-8
Item No. 304394

TABLE OF CONTENTS - *The Outsiders*

ABOUT THE AUTHOR
S. E. HINTON

HINTON, S. E. Susan Eloise Hinton was born on July 22, 1948 in Tulsa, Oklahoma. In her junior year at Will Rogers High School in Tulsa (at the age of 17) she wrote *The Outsiders*, the book that sent the young adult book world on an entirely new path.

The Outsiders contained some characters and places based on people and places Ms. Hinton knew or knew of, but as with most great writers of fiction, S.E. Hinton used her knowledge of people and places and wove them into a tale of fiction that transcended a specific time and place and mirrored the truths of a part of our society.

The Outsiders was just the beginning. In 1971 *That Was Then, This Is Now* was published, followed by *Rumblefish* in 1975, *Tex* in 1979, and *Taming the Star Runner* in 1988.

In 1970 S.E. Hinton married David Inhofe, and in 1983 their son Nicholas David was born.

INTRODUCTION

This unit has been designed to develop students' reading, writing, thinking, and language skills through exercises and activities related to *The Outsiders* by S. E. Hinton. It includes eighteen lessons, supported by extra resource materials.

The **introductory lesson** introduces students to one main theme of the novel through a game-type activity. Following the introductory activity, students are given a transition to explain how the activity relates to the book they are about to read. Following the transition, students are given the materials they will be using during the unit. At the end of the lesson, students begin the pre-reading work for the first reading assignment.

The **reading assignments** are approximately thirty pages each; some are a little shorter while others are a little longer. Students have approximately 15 minutes of pre-reading work to do prior to each reading assignment. This pre-reading work involves reviewing the study questions for the assignment and doing some vocabulary work for 8 to 10 vocabulary words they will encounter in their reading.

The **study guide questions** are fact-based questions; students can find the answers to these questions right in the text. These questions come in two formats: short answer or multiple choice The best use of these materials is probably to use the short answer version of the questions as study guides for students (since answers will be more complete), and to use the multiple choice version for occasional quizzes. If your school has the appropriate machinery, it might be a good idea to make transparencies of your answer keys for the overhead projector.

The **vocabulary work** is intended to enrich students' vocabularies as well as to aid in the students' understanding of the book. Prior to each reading assignment, students will complete a two-part worksheet for approximately 8 to 10 vocabulary words in the upcoming reading assignment. Part I focuses on students' use of general knowledge and contextual clues by giving the sentence in which the word appears in the text. Students are then to write down what they think the words mean based on the words' usage. Part II nails down the definitions of the words by giving students dictionary definitions of the words and having students match the words to the correct definitions based on the words' contextual usage. Students should then have a thorough understanding of the words when they meet them in the text.

After each reading assignment, students will go back and formulate answers for the study guide questions. Discussion of these questions serves as a review of the most important events and ideas presented in the reading assignments.

A lesson is devoted to the **extra discussion questions/writing assignments**. These questions focus on interpretation, critical analysis and personal response, employing a variety of thinking skills and adding to the students' understanding of the novel.

Following the discussion of the novel, there is a **vocabulary review** lesson which pulls together all of the fragmented vocabulary lists for the reading assignments and gives students a review of all of the words they have studied.

There is a **group activity** that will have students working in small groups to plan and carry out ways in which to improve their neighborhoods.

There are **three writing assignments** in this unit, each with the purpose of informing, persuading, or having students express personal opinions. The first assignment is to express personal opinions: students write the same composition that Pony was assigned to write. The second assignment is to persuade: after watching the movie of *The Outsiders*, students are to complete a worksheet comparing and contrasting the movie and the book. Based on those observations and employing their own personal opinions, students are to persuade their audiences to either read the book or watch the movie (whichever they think would be better). The third assignment is to inform: students will write a report in which they inform the teacher of the purpose, progress and conclusions of their neighborhood improvement group activity.

In addition, there is a **nonfiction reading assignment**. Students are required to read a piece of nonfiction related in some way to *The Outsiders* (articles about problems in the city, street gangs, kids who essentially live on their own without any parental supervision, heroes, daring rescues, reports of local fires--past or current--, accounts of senseless or accidental murders, etc.). After reading their nonfiction pieces, students will fill out a worksheet on which they answer questions regarding facts, interpretation, criticism, and personal opinions. During one class period, students make **oral presentations** about the nonfiction pieces they have read. This not only exposes all students to a wealth of information, it also gives students the opportunity to practice **public speaking.**

The **review lesson** pulls together all of the aspects of the unit. The teacher is given four or five choices of activities or games to use which all serve the same basic function of reviewing all of the information presented in the unit.

The **unit test** comes in two formats: multiple choice or short answer. As a convenience, two different tests for each format have been included.

There are **additional support materials** included with this unit. The extra activities section includes suggestions for an in-class library, crossword and word search puzzles related to the novel, and extra vocabulary worksheets. There is a list of bulletin board ideas which gives the teacher suggestions for bulletin boards to go along with this unit. In addition, there is a list of extra class activities the teacher could choose from to enhance the unit or as a substitution for an exercise the teacher might feel is inappropriate for his/her class. Answer keys follow the reproducible student materials, which may be reproduced for use in the teacher's classroom without infringement of copyrights. No other portion of the unit may be reproduced without the written consent of Teacher's Pet Publications, Inc.

UNIT OBJECTIVES - *The Outsiders*

1. Through reading Hinton's *The Outsiders*, students will consider the importance of judging people as individuals rather than as members of groups.

2. Students will demonstrate their understanding of the text on four levels: factual, interpretive, critical and personal.

3. Students will take time to focus on their own neighborhoods and ways in which they could be improved.

4. Students will study passages from the story to extract the themes and to further study the author's use of language.

5. Students will be given the opportunity to practice reading aloud and silently to improve their skills in each area.

6. Students will answer questions to demonstrate their knowledge and understanding of the main events and characters in *The Outsiders* as they relate to the author's theme development.

7. Students will enrich their vocabularies and improve their understanding of the novel through the vocabulary lessons prepared for use in conjunction with the novel.

8. The writing assignments in this unit are geared to several purposes:
   a. To have students demonstrate their abilities to inform, to persuade, or to express their own personal ideas
      > Note: Students will demonstrate ability to write effectively to <u>inform</u> by developing and organizing facts to convey information. Students will demonstrate the ability to write effectively to <u>persuade</u> by selecting and organizing relevant information, establishing an argumentative purpose, and by designing an appropriate strategy for an identified audience. Students will demonstrate the ability to write effectively to <u>express personal ideas</u> by selecting a form and its appropriate elements.
   b. To check the students' reading comprehension
   c. To make students think about the ideas presented by the novel
   d. To encourage logical thinking
   e. To provide an opportunity to practice good grammar and improve students' use of the English language

9. Students will read aloud, report, and participate in large and small group discussions to improve their public speaking and personal interaction skills.

READING ASSIGNMENT SHEET - *The Outsiders*

Date Assigned	Reading Assignment (Chapters)	Completion Date
	1-2	
	3-4	
	5-6	
	7-9	
	10-12	

UNIT OUTLINE - *The Outsiders*

1	2	3	4	5
Introduction PV 1-2	Read 1-2	Study ?s 1-2 PVR 3-4	Study ?s 3-4 PVR 5-6	Group Project
6	**7**	**8**	**9**	**10**
Study ?s 5-6 PVR 7-9	Quiz/?s 7-9 PVR 10-12	Study ?s 10-12 Writing Assignment 1	Extra Discussion Questions	Discussion
11	**12**	**13**	**14**	**15**
Vocabulary	Quotations Nonfiction Reading	Movie Writing Conf.	Movie Writing Conf.	Writing Assignment 2
16	**17**	**18**	**19**	**20**
Writing Assignment 3	Nonfiction Reports	Group Writing Assignment	Review	Test

Key: P = Preview Study Questions   V = Vocabulary Work   R = Read

STUDY GUIDE QUESTIONS

STUDY GUIDE QUESTIONS - *The Outsiders*

Chapters 1-2
1. Identify Darry, Soda and Ponyboy.
2. How are Greasers different from Socs?
3. Who were other members of Pony's gang?
4. What happened to Pony on his way home from the movies?
5. Who did Dally, Johnny and Ponyboy meet at the Nightly Double?
6. Contrast Dally's approach to Cherry and Marcia with Pony's, and contrast Cherry's response to Dally with her response to Pony.
7. Why were Cherry and Marcia alone at the drive-in?
8. Pony was somewhat surprised that he was getting along with Cherry and Marcia. Why?
9. What had happened to Johnny prior to the time of this story?

Chapters 3-4
1. After talking with Cherry, what reason does Pony finally give for the separation between Greasers and Socs?
2. Who were Cherry and Marcia's boyfriends?
3. Why didn't the Socs and Greasers fight during their first encounter after the movie?
4. Why was Pony late coming home from the Nightly Double?
5. What caused Pony to "run away"?
6. What happened to Johnny and Ponyboy at the park?
7. To whom do Johnny and Pony turn for help after Johnny killed Bob? Why?
8. Why did Johnny and Pony go to Jay's Mountain?

Chapters 5-6
1. Why was Pony upset about getting a haircut?
2. What was Johnny's favorite part of *Gone With the Wind*? Of whom did it remind him?
3. When Dally finally arrives at the church, what news does he bring?
4. What did Johnny announce after his fifth barbecue sandwich?
5. Describe Johnny's relationship with his parents.
6. What happened when Johnny, Pony and Dally returned to the church?

Chapters 7-9

1. What additional problem did the three brothers face after Pony's return?
2. Why did Randy want to talk to Pony?
3. When Johnny's mother came to visit him at the hospital, what was Johnny's reaction?
4. Why wouldn't Cherry go visit Johnny?
5. Compare and contrast the boys' reasons for fighting. (Darry, Steve, Soda and Two-Bit)
6. What did Pony say was the difference between Tim's gang and his?
7. Identify Paul Holden.
8. Who "won" the rumble?
9. Where did Dally take Pony after the rumble?
10. How do we know Dally felt at least partially responsible for Johnny's fate?
11. What advice did Dally give to Pony on the way to the hospital after the rumble?
12. What were Johnny's last words to Ponyboy?

Chapters 10-12

1. Of what did Pony try to convince himself on the way home from the hospital?
2. What did Pony decide was the reason Dally couldn't take Johnny's death?
3. Why did Dally rob the grocery store and then raise his unloaded gun to the police?
4. Why would Pony have thought he was in Windrixville while he was delirious?
5. What was Pony's reaction when Randy talked about Johnny?
6. What was the result of the court hearing?
7. How did Pony react to the three Socs who bullied him about killing Bob?
8. Johnny's note made several points. What were they?
9. How do we know Ponyboy will be all right?

Chapters 1-2

1. Identify Darry, Soda and Ponyboy.
> They are orphaned brothers who live alone on the East Side. They are "Greasers,"
> members of a gang of friends who look out for each other.

2. How are Greasers different from Socs?
> Greasers are from the east side of town. They are poor and usually in trouble with the
> law. Socs (Socials) are from the west side of town. They come from wealthy families and
> have fancy cars and parties.

3. Who were other members of Pony's gang?
> Darry, Soda, Two-Bit, Johnny, Dally, and Steve

4. What happened to Pony on his way home from the movies?
> He was jumped by some Socs. He was not seriously injured because his friends came
> along and ran off the Socs.

5. Who did Dally, Johnny and Ponyboy meet at the Nightly Double?
> They met Cherry and Marcia, two Soc girls.

6. Contrast Dally's approach to Cherry and Marcia with Pony's, and contrast Cherry's response
   to Dally with her response to Pony.
> Dally was rude, crude, foul-mouthed and annoying to the girls. Pony was polite, sensitive
> and rather soft-spoken. Cherry insulted and rejected Dally but accepted Pony's friendship.

7. Why were Cherry and Marcia alone at the drive-in?
> The girls had a fight with their boyfriends, who left.

8. Pony was somewhat surprised that he was getting along with Cherry and Marcia. Why?
> They were Socs; he was a Greaser. No Soc girls had ever spoken to him except to insult
> him.

9. What had happened to Johnny prior to the time of this story?
> He had been jumped and beaten by a group of Socs who came from a blue Mustang.

Chapters 3-4

1. After talking with Cherry, what reason does Pony finally give for the separation between
   Greasers and Socs?
> "It's not money, it's feeling--you don't feel anything and we feel too violently."

2. Who were Cherry and Marcia's boyfriends?

> They are Bob and Randy, two of the Socs who beat up Johnny. Bob had a blue Mustang and wore rings.

3. Why didn't the Socs and Greasers fight during their first encounter after the movie?

> The Socs were interested in getting their girlfriends back. The boys knew the girls did not like fights, so they didn't fight. Also, it helped that the girls went along with them willingly. Had the girls protested, the Soc boys may have fought.

4. Why was Pony late coming home from the Nightly Double?

> He and Johnny stopped to look at the stars and talk, and they fell asleep.

5. What caused Pony to "run away" ?

> Darry hit him during an argument over his being late.

6. What happened to Johnny and Ponyboy at the park?

> The Socs in the blue Mustang found them. They tried to drown Ponyboy in the fountain. Johnny got scared and stabbed Bob, killing him. The other Socs fled.

7. To whom do Johnny and Pony turn for help after Johnny killed Bob? Why?

> They turn to Dally because he has experience at such things. Also, both Johnny's parents and Pony's brothers would have been of no help,

8. Why did Johnny and Pony go to Jay's Mountain?

> There was an old church there where the boys could hide out until Dally could come with the next part of a plan.

Chapters 5-6

1. Why was Pony upset about getting a haircut?

> "It was my pride. . . . Our hair labeled us Greasers, too -- it was our trademark. The one thing we were proud of. Maybe we couldn't have Corvairs or madras shirts, but we could have hair."

2. What was Johnny's favorite part of *Gone With the Wind*? Of whom did it remind him?

> He especially liked the gallant Southern gentlemen. They reminded him of Dally.

3. When Dally finally arrives at the church, what news does he bring?

> He tells the boys that the police are looking for them towards Texas. He brings a note from Soda to Pony. He also tells them that the Socs and Greasers are supposed to have a rumble the next night and that Cherry is a spy for the Greasers.

4. What did Johnny announce after his fifth barbecue sandwich?

> He wanted them to go back and turn themselves in to the police.

5. Describe Johnny's relationship with his parents.

They ignored him or beat him up all of the time. He wanted them to take a personal interest in him and would have liked to please them, but they don't respond. They don't even ask for Johnny when he disappears after killing Bob.

6. What happened when Johnny, Pony and Dally returned to the church?

The church had caught on fire. Johnny and Pony went in to get some children out of the burning building. Pony got out with minor injuries. Dally went in to get Johnny, who had severe burns and a broken back. Dally came out with Johnny, an injured arm and burns.

Chapters 7-9

1. What additional problem did the three brothers face after Pony's return?

They faced the possibility of being separated into foster homes.

2. Why did Randy want to talk to Pony?

He wanted to tell him that he would not be at the rumble, to try to call off the rumble by convincing Pony that there could be no winner.

3. When Johnny's mother came to visit him at the hospital, what was Johnny's reaction?

He rejects her visit; he tells the nurse he does not want to see his mother.

4. Why wouldn't Cherry go visit Johnny?

"He killed Bob. . . . I could never look at the person who killed him."

5. Compare and contrast the boys' reasons for fighting. (Darry, Steve, Soda and Two-Bit)

Darry fights for pride (to show off his strength); Steve fights for hatred (to stomp the other guy); Soda fights for fun (a contest); Two-Bit fights for conformity (Everyone fights.).

6. What did Pony say was the difference between Tim's gang and his?

". . . they had a leader and were organized; we were just buddies who stuck together–each man was his own leader."

7. Identify Paul Holden.

Paul was Darry's old football team buddy. He stepped up to begin the rumble representing the Socs against Darry who represented the Greasers. He threw the first punch when Darry wasn't looking.

8. Who "won" the rumble?

The Greasers "won."

9. Where did Dally take Pony after the rumble?

He took him to the hospital to see Johnny.

10. How do we know Dally felt at least partially responsible for Johnny's fate?
> He said, "I was crazy, you know that, kid? Crazy for wantin' Johnny to stay outa trouble, for not wantin' him to get hard. If he'd been like me he'd never have run into that church." Also, remember that Dally sent the boys to the church in the first place.

11. What advice did Dally give to Pony on the way to the hospital after the rumble?
> ". . . You'd better wise up, Pony . . . you get tough like me and you don't get hurt. You look out for yourself and nothing can touch you."

12. What were Johnny's last words to Ponyboy?
> "Stay gold, Ponyboy. Stay gold. . . ."

Chapters 10-12
1. Of what did Pony try to convince himself on the way home from the hospital?
> He tried to convince himself that Johnny was not dead.

2. What did Pony decide was the reason Dally couldn't take Johnny's death?
> "Johnny was the only thing Dally loved."

3. Why did Dally rob the grocery store and then raise his unloaded gun to the police?
> ". . . Dally Winston wanted to be dead. . . ."

4. Why would Pony have thought he was in Windrixville while he was delirious?
> It was the time before Johnny and Dally died. He didn't want to face up to their deaths.

5. What was Pony's reaction when Randy talked about Johnny?
> He said, "I had the knife. I killed Bob. . . . Johnny is not dead."

6. What was the result of the court hearing?
> Pony was acquitted and the case was closed.

7. How did Pony react to the three Socs who bullied him about killing Bob?
> He busted off the end of a bottle and said, "You get back in your car or you'll get split." And he meant it.

8. Johnny's note made several points. What were they?
> He didn't mind dying for those kids. Pony should stay gold -- never become jaded. Pony still has time to make whatever life he wants for himself. There is still good in the world. "Tell Dally."

9. How do we know Ponyboy will be all right?

He says he realizes that Johnny killed Bob and that Johnny and Dally are dead. We can see that Johnny's note had a positive effect on Pony. And we are led to believe that he wrote the story and has put the events into perspective in his life.

MULTIPLE CHOICE STUDY GUIDE/QUIZ QUESTIONS - *The Outsiders*

Chapters 1-2

Place the letter(s) of the correct answer(s) in the blanks provided.

A = Pony B = Darry C = Soda D = Johnny E = Two-Bit F = Steve
G = Cherry & Marcia H = Socs I = Greasers J = Dally

_____ 1. They were orphaned brothers who live on the East side.

_____ 2. This gang came from the West side. The members are wealthy.

_____ 3. Who were the members of Pony's gang?

_____ 4. Pony was jumped by them on his way home from the movies.

_____ 5. Who did Dally, Johnny & Pony meet at the Nightly Double?

_____ 6. He was rude, crude, foul-mouthed and annoyed the girls.

_____ 7. He was polite and soft-spoken, and Cherry accepted his friendship.

_____ 8. Pony was surprised the girls were being nice to him because they were ___.

_____ 9. Some of them drove a blue Mustang.

_____ 10. This gang came from the East side.

<u>Chapters 3-4</u>
1. After talking with Cherry, what reason does Pony finally give for the separation between Greasers and Socs?
      a. money
      b. education
      c. feelings
      d. background

2. Who were Cherry and Marcia's boyfriends?
      a. Bob and Randy
      b. Dally and Bob
      c. Randy and Steve
      d. Steve and Dally

3. Why didn't the Socs and Greasers fight during their first encounter after the movie?
      a. The Socs wanted their girlfriends back.
      b. The girls did not like fighting.
      c. The girls went willingly.
      d. All of the above

4. Why was Pony late coming home from the Nightly Double?
      a. He and Johnny fell asleep at the movie.
      b. He got into a fight.
      c. He and Johnny fell asleep looking at the stars.
      d. They were busy talking to Cherry.

5. What caused Pony to "run away" ?
      a. Darry hit him.
      b. Cherry asked him to go with her.
      c. He wanted a better life.
      d. He was scared.

6. What did Johnny do at the park?
      a. He fell asleep.
      b. He stabbed Bob.
      c. He drowned.
      d. He drowned Bob.

7. To whom do Johnny and Pony turn for help after Johnny killed Bob? Why?
      a. Cherry
      b. Darry
      c. Dally
      d. Two-Bit

8. Why did Johnny and Pony go to Jay's Mountain?
      a. to hide out in the back woods
      b. to hide out at the church there
      c. to get across the state line
      d. to meet Two-Bit

Chapters 5-6

1. Why was Pony upset about getting a haircut?
    a. He was proud of his hair.
    b. He hated wearing hats.
    c. It was his trademark as a greaser.
    d. A & C

2. What was Johnny's favorite part of *Gone With the Wind*?
    a. He liked the gallant Southern gentlemen.
    b. He could identify with Scarlett's attachment to the land.
    c. He liked the battle scenes.
    d. He liked when Rhett told Scarlett off.

3. When Dally finally arrives at the church, what news does he bring?
    a. The police are looking for them towards Texas.
    b. Cherry is a spy for the Greasers.
    c. The Socs and Greasers are having a rumble the next night.
    d. All of the above

4. What did Johnny announce after his fifth barbecue sandwich?
    a. He was stuffed full and had never had such delicious food.
    b. He was ready for part two of their plan.
    c. He wanted them to go back and turn themselves in.
    d. He was going to throw up.

5. Describe Johnny's relationship with his parents.
    a. His parents were a close loving family.
    b. His parents ignored him and beat him up.
    c. Johnny hated his parents but they loved him.
    d. Johnny didn't care about his parents and they didn't care about him.

6. What happened when Johnny, Pony and Dally returned to the church?
    a. The preacher found them.
    b. The police had surrounded the building and were waiting for them.
    c. They blew up the church.
    d. The church had caught on fire.

<u>Chapters 7-9</u>

1. What additional problem did the three brothers face after Pony's return?
    a. They might be separated into foster homes.
    b. They had been kicked out of their home.
    c. They had to go to a detention center.
    d. Darry lost his job and could no longer support them.

2. Why did Randy want to talk to Pony?
    a. He wanted to tell Pony to leave Cherry alone.
    b. He wanted to gloat about Johnny's death.
    c. He wanted to try to call off the rumble.
    d. He wanted to offer Pony a job.

3. When Johnny's mother came to visit him at the hospital, what was Johnny's reaction?
    a. He rejects her.
    b. He is overjoyed.
    c. He has to be physically restrained to keep from hitting her.
    d. He throws his tray of food at her.

4. Why wouldn't Cherry go visit Johnny?
    a. She couldn't make time to go see him. She was too busy.
    b. She was afraid she'd try to kill him.
    c. Johnny killed Bob; she couldn't stand to look at Johnny.
    d. She couldn't stand hospitals.

5. Match the reason for fighting to the correct character:
    ___ Darry   a. fun
    ___ Steve   b. hatred
    ___ Soda   c. pride
    ___ Two-Bit   d. conformity

6. What did Pony say was the difference between Tim's gang and his?
    a. Pony's gang was organized and had a leader.
    b. Tim's gang was organized and had a leader.
    c. Tim's gang was just buddies who stuck together.
    d. Tim's gang was more desperate.

7. Identify Paul Holden.
    a. He tried to call off the rumble at the last minute.
    b. He was Cherry's new boyfriend.
    c. He was Pony's friend.
    d. He was Darry's old football team buddy who threw the first
       punch in the final rumble.

8. Who "won" the rumble?
    a. Socs
    b. Greasers
    c. No one

9. Where did Dally take Pony after the rumble?
    a. to the hospital emergency room
    b. to the movies
    c. to the hospital to see Johnny
    d. home

10. How do we know Dally felt at least partially responsible for Johnny's fate?
    a. He taught Johnny about the importance of being heroic.
    b. He kept Johnny from becoming "hard.."
    c. He forced his ideas about putting others before yourself onto Johnny.
    d. None of the above

11. What advice did Dally give to Pony on the way to the hospital after the rumble?
    a. "Get tough like me and you won't get hurt."
    b. "Do unto other as you want them to do unto you."
    c. "Move away while you can."
    d. "Revenge is always best."

12. What were Johnny's last words to Ponyboy?
    a. "Tell my mother I'm sorry."
    b. "Have a rumble for me."
    c. "Remember to look out for yourself, Ponyboy."
    d. "Stay gold, Ponyboy. Stay gold...."

Chapters 10-12

1. Of what did Pony try to convince himself on the way home from the hospital?
   a. It was important to be a member of a gang.
   b. He could get along with the Socs.
   c. Johnny was not dead.
   d. Things would be different but better.

2. What did Pony decide was the reason Dally couldn't take Johnny's death?
   a. Johnny was the only thing Dally loved.
   b. Dally couldn't deal with any death.
   c. Dally couldn't ever handle reality.
   d. Dally made Johnny go back into the burning building and was therefore the cause of Johnny's death

3. Why did Dally rob the grocery store and then raise his unloaded gun to the police?
   a. Dally was a dare-devil always testing the limits of his power.
   b. Dally was just an ordinary criminal.
   c. Dally wanted to be shot.
   d. Dally forgot his gun was unloaded.

4. Why would Pony have thought he was in Windrixville while he was delirious?
   a. That's where his grandparents were
   b. He didn't want to face up to Johnny's or Dally's death.
   c. It was his childhood home.
   d. None of the above

5. What was Pony's reaction when Randy talked about Johnny?
   a. He told Randy to shut up.
   b. He began to cry.
   c. He hit Randy.
   d. He told Randy that he had killed Bob and Johnny was not dead.

6. What was the result of the court hearing?
   a. Pony was acquitted.
   b. Pony was found guilty.
   c. Darry was found guilty as the guardian of Pony, since Pony was a minor and the boys were sent to a reform school.
   d. The boys were sent to foster homes.

7. How did Pony react to the three Socs who bullied him about killing Bob?
     a. He ignored them.
     b. He began to cry.
     c. He busted a bottle and threatened them.
     d. He ran away.

8. Johnny's note made several points. Which one was <u>NOT</u> one of Johnny's points?
     a. There is still good in the world.
     b. He didn't mind dying for those kids.
     c. Pony can make whatever he wants of his life.
     d. He forgives his mother and father.

9. How do we know Ponyboy will be all right?
     a. He wrote the story and has put the events into perspective in his life.
     b. He realizes Johnny killed Bob.
     c. He realizes that Johnny and Dally are dead.
     d. All of the above

ANSWER KEY MULTIPLE CHOICE STUDY/QUIZ QUESTIONS
The Outsiders

Chapters 1-2	Chapters 3-4	Chapters 5-6	Chapters 7-9	Chapters 10-12
1. A B C	1. C	1. D	1. A	1. C
2. H	2. A	2. A	2. C	2. A
3. A B C	3. D	3. C	3. A	3. C
D E F J				
4. H	4. C	4. C	4. C	4. B
5. G	5. A	5. B	5. C	5. D
6. J	6. B	6. B	B	6. A
7. A	7. C		A	7. C
8. H	8. B		D	8. D
9. H			6. B	9. D
10. I			7. D	
			8. B	
			9. C	
			10. B	
			11. A	
			12. D	

PREREADING VOCABULARY
WORKSHEETS

VOCABULARY - *The Outsiders*

Chapters 1-3 Part I: Using Prior Knowledge and Contextual Clues
     Below are the sentences in which the vocabulary words appear in the text. Read the sentence. Use any clues you can find in the sentence combined with your prior knowledge, and write what you think the underlined words mean on the lines provided.

1. I have to be <u>content</u> with what I have.

_____

2. I am a greaser and most of my neighborhood <u>rarely</u> bothers to get a haircut.

_____

3. I thought I was the only person in the world that did. So I <u>loned</u> it.

_____

4. Not like the Socs, who jump greasers and wreck houses and throw beer blasts for kicks, and get editorials in the paper for being a public disgrace one day and an <u>asset</u> to society the next.

_____

5. I automatically hitched my thumbs in my jeans and <u>slouched,</u> wondering if I could get away if I made a break for it.

_____

6. He had on a <u>madras</u> shirt.

_____

7. He has dark-brown hair that kicks out in front and a slight <u>cowlick</u> in the back-just like Dad's...

_____

8. I drew a <u>quivering</u> breath and quit crying.

_____

9. Steve Randle was seventeen, tall and lean, with thick greasy hair he kept combed in <u>complicated</u> swirls.

_____

10. "Sure," I said, trying for Soda's sake to keep the <u>sarcasm</u> out of my voice.

_____

11. She gave him an <u>incredulous</u> look; and then she threw her Coke in his face.

_____

12. "Okay," I said <u>nonchalantly</u>, "might as well."

_____

Part II: Determining the Meaning

    Match the vocabulary words to their dictionary definitions. If there are words for which you cannot figure out the definition by contextual clues and by process of elimination, look them up in a dictionary.

___ 1. content	A. worth
___ 2. rarely	B. indifferently
___ 3. loned	C. tuft of hair growing in a different direction
___ 4. asset	D. unbelieving
___ 5. slouched	E. trembling, shaking
___ 6. madras	F. bitter cutting jest
___ 7. cowlick	G. by oneself
___ 8. quivering	H. an ungainly gait
___ 9. complicated	I. satisfied, pleased
___ 10. sarcasm	J. uncommon, infrequent
___ 11. incredulous	K. involved, complex
___ 12. nonchalantly	L. cotton fabric shirt usually bright colored

Vocabulary - *The Outsiders* Chapters 3-4

Part I: Using Prior Knowledge and Contextual Clues
    Below are the sentences in which the vocabulary words appear in the text. Read the sentence. Use any clues you can find in the sentence combined with your prior knowledge, and write what you think the underlined words mean on the lines provided.

1. You're more emotional. We're sophisticated - cool to the point of not feeling anything.

_____

2. "And," Two-Bit added grimly, "A few other of the socially elite checkered-shirt set."

_____

3. "Well," Cherry said resignedly, "they've spotted us."

_____

4. My teeth chattered unceasingly and I couldn't stop them.

_____

5. Buck . . . made most of his money on fixed races and a little bootlegging.

_____

6. He was pretty well crocked, which made me apprehensive.

_____

7. "Oh, shoot, kid" -Dally glanced contemptuously over his shoulder-"I was in the bedroom."

_____

8. He winced at the pain in his legs.

_____

9. . . . I thought with a bewildering feeling of being rushed, things are happening too quick.

_____

10. But this church gave me a kind of creepy feeling. What do you call it? Premonition?

_____

Vocabulary - *The Outsiders* Chapters 3-4 Continued

Part II: Determining the Meaning -- Match the vocabulary words to their definitions.

___ 13. sarcasm   A. to shrink back as from pain

___ 14. incredulous   B. confused, perplexed

___ 15. nonchalantly   C. scornful, insolent

___ 16. sophisticated   D. giving up, accepting the future

___ 17. elite   E. bitter cutting jest

___ 18. resignedly   F. cultured, worldly

___ 19. unceasingly   G. indifferently

___ 20. bootlegging   H. previous warning, information, feeling

___ 21. apprehensive   I. unbelieving

___ 22. contemptuously   J. continual

___ 23. winced   K. a select body, the best

___ 24. bewildering   L. afraid, suspicious

___ 25. premonition   M. selling alcohol where not legally available

Vocabulary - *The Outsiders* Chapters 5-6

Part I: Using Prior Knowledge and Contextual Clues
     Below are the sentences in which the vocabulary words appear in the text. Read the sentence. Use any clues you can find in the sentence combined with your prior knowledge, and write what you think the underlined words mean on the lines provided.

1. I had never slept so soundly. I was still <u>groggy</u>.

_____

2. "Gee, thanks." I put the book down <u>reluctantly</u>. I wanted to start it right then.

_____

3. I looked at Johnny <u>imploringly</u>.

_____

4. I leaned back next to him <u>sullenly</u>. "I guess so."

_____

5. I was trying to find the meaning the poet had in mind, but it <u>eluded</u> me.

_____

6. And it suddenly became real and <u>vital</u>.

_____

7. "You're starved?" Johnny was so <u>indignant</u> he nearly squeaked.

_____

8. Johnny and I <u>gorged</u> on barbecue sandwiches and banana splits.

_____

9. "I was scared," Johnny said with <u>conviction</u>.

_____

10. You just keeled over from smoke <u>inhalation</u> and a little shock . . . .

_____

Vocabulary - *The Outsiders* Chapters 5-6 Continued

Part II: Determining the Meaning -- Match the vocabulary words to their definitions.

___ 26. groggy   A. strong belief
___ 27. reluctantly   B. essential, necessary to life
___ 28. imploringly   C. escaped, avoided
___ 29. sullenly   D. swallow with greediness
___ 30. eluded   E. beseechingly
___ 31. vital   F. not fully awake
___ 32. indignant   G. to breathe into the lungs
___ 33. gorged   H. gloomily, somber
___ 34. conviction   I. unwillingly, struggling against
___ 35. inhalation   J. disgusted, anger with contempt

Vocabulary - *The Outsiders* Chapters 7-8

Part I: Using Prior Knowledge and Contextual Clues
        Below are the sentences in which the vocabulary words appear in the text. Read the sentence. Use any clues you can find in the sentence combined with your prior knowledge, and write what you think the underlined words mean on the lines provided.

1. He'd . . . walk around interviewing the nurses and <u>mimicking</u> T.V. reporters.

_____

2. . . . . it stopped <u>recurring</u> so often, but it happened often enough for Darry to take me to a
    doctor.

_____

3. "Work?" Two-Bit was <u>aghast</u>. "And ruin my rep?"

_____

4. Two-Bit was telling me about one of his many <u>exploits</u> while we did the dishes.

_____

5. Turning <u>abruptly</u>, he said, "Let's go see Dallas."

_____

6. She was a little woman, with straight black hair and big, black eyes like Johnny's. But that
    was as far as the <u>resemblance</u> went.

_____

7. I could tell that he was <u>debating</u> whether to tell Dally the truth or not.

_____

8. It was the reward of two hours of walking <u>aimlessly</u> around a hardware store to divert
    suspicion.

_____

Vocabulary - *The Outsiders* Chapters 7-8 Continued

9. Tim grinned <u>ruefully</u> probably thinking of his roughneck, hard-headed brother.

_____

10. We mostly stuck with our own outfits, so I was a little <u>leery</u> of going over to him.

_____

Part II: Determining the Meaning -- Match the vocabulary words to their definitions.

___ 36. mimicking
___ 37. recurring
___ 38. aghast
___ 39. exploits
___ 40. abruptly
___ 41. resemblance
___ 42. debating
___ 43. aimlessly
___ 44. ruefully
___ 45. leery

A. heroic acts, adventures
B. regretfully, sorrowfully
C. wary, suspicious
D. likeness, similarity
E. without direction, without purpose
F. imitating, ridiculing
G. returning, repeatedly
H. suddenly
I. deciding
J. amazed, stupefied

Vocabulary - *The Outsiders* Chapters 10-12

Part I: Using Prior Knowledge and Contextual Clues

     Below are the sentences in which the vocabulary words appear in the text. Read the sentence. Use any clues you can find in the sentence combined with your prior knowledge, and write what you think the underlined words mean on the lines provided.

1. Dally had taken the car and I started the long walk home in a <u>stupor</u>, Johnny was dead.

_____

2. He died violent and young and <u>desperate</u>, just like we all knew he'd die someday.

_____

3. But I had a sick feeling that maybe I hadn't called for him while I was <u>delirious</u>, maybe I had only wanted Sodapop to be with me.

_____

4. Soda never has <u>grasped</u> the importance Darry and I put on athletics.

_____

5. He grinned but didn't <u>deny</u> it.

_____

6. I'd rather have anybody's hate than their <u>pity</u>.

_____

7. "Yes, sir," looking straight at the judge, not <u>flinching</u>;

_____

8. Then he said I was <u>acquitted</u> and the whole case was closed.

_____

9. He <u>veered</u> off to the right, but I caught him in a flying tackle before he'd gone more than a couple of steps.

___

Part II: Determining the Meaning -- Match the vocabulary words to their definitions.

___ 46. stupor   A. confusedly

___ 47. delirious   B. swerved, turned aside from a course or direction

___ 48. grasped   C. driven to take any risk

___ 49. acquitted   D. to declare untrue; contradict

___ 50. desperate   E. understood

___ 51. bewilderdly   F. senses are deadened

___ 52. deny   G. discharged completed, set free from a legal charge

___ 53. pity   H. betraying fear, pain or surprise with an
                                     involuntary gesture

___ 54. flinching   I.   compassion for suffering

___ 55. veered   J. confusion, disordered speech, hallucinations

VOCABULARY ANSWER KEY - *The Outsiders*

Chapters 1-2	Chapters 3-4	Chapters 5-6	Chapters 7-9	Chapters 10-12
1. I	13. E	26. F	36. F	46. F
2. J	14. I	27. I	37. G	47. J
3. G	15. G	28. E	38. J	48. E
4. A	16. F	29. H	39. A	49. G
5. H	17. K	30. C	40. H	50. C
6. L	18. D	31. B	41. D	51. A
7. C	19. J	32. J	42. I	52. D
8. E	20. M	33. D	43. E	53. I
9. K	21. L	34. A	44. B	54. H
10. F	22. C	35. G	45. C	55. B
11. D	23. A			
12. B	24. B			
	25. H			

DAILY LESSONS

LESSON ONE

Objectives
> 1. To introduce the unit
> 2. To distribute books and other related materials
> 3. To preview the study questions for chapters 1-2
> 4. To familiarize students with the vocabulary for chapters 1-2

NOTE: You need to have students bring in pictures of their heroes--people they admire (or something which represents their heroes).

Also as prior preparation, you should put up the background paper and title for a bulletin board entitled DID I EVER TELL YOU YOU'RE MY HERO? or some other suitable phrase. Leave space for students to post their pictures.

Activity #1

Ask students to clear their desks except for the pictures they brought to class. Have each student explain what his (her) picture represents and then let the student post it on the bulletin board.

Explain that most people need someone to look up to, someone they respect to give them praise and guidance. *The Outsiders* is a book about gang rivalry, the needs and wants of the individual members of the gangs, and the question of "who is a hero?"

Activity #2

Distribute the materials students will use in this unit. Explain in detail how students are to use these materials.

Study Guides Students should read the study guide questions for each reading assignment prior to beginning the reading assignment to get a feeling for what events and ideas are important in the section they are about to read. After reading the section, students will (as a class or individually) answer the questions to review the important events and ideas from that section of the book. Students should keep the study guides as study materials for the unit test.

Vocabulary Prior to reading a reading assignment, students will do vocabulary work related to the section of the book they are about to read. Following the completion of the reading of the book, there will be a vocabulary review of all the words used in the vocabulary assignments. Students should keep their vocabulary work as study materials for the unit test.

Reading Assignment Sheet   You need to fill in the reading assignment sheet to let students know by when their reading has to be completed. You can either write the assignment sheet up on a side blackboard or bulletin board and leave it there for students to see each day, or you can "ditto" copies for each student to have. In either case, you should advise students to become very familiar with the reading assignments so they know what is expected of them.

Extra Activities Center   The Extra Activities section of this unit contains suggestions for an extra library of related books and articles in your classroom as well as crossword and word search puzzles. Make an extra activities center in your room where you will keep these materials for students to use. (Bring the books and articles in from the library and keep several copies of the puzzles on hand.) Explain to students that these materials are available for students to use when they finish reading assignments or other class work early.

Nonfiction Assignment Sheet   Explain to students that they each are to read at least one non-fiction piece from the in-class library at some time during the unit. Students will fill out a nonfiction assignment sheet after completing the reading to help you evaluate their reading experiences and to help the students think about and evaluate their own reading experiences.

Books   Each school has its own rules and regulations regarding student use of school books. Advise students of the procedures that are normal for your school.

Activity #3
Preview the study questions and have students do the vocabulary work for Chapters 1-2 of *The Outsiders*. If students do not finish this assignment during this class period, they should complete it prior to the next class meeting.

NONFICTION ASSIGNMENT SHEET
(To be completed after reading the required nonfiction article)

Name _____ Date _____

Title of Nonfiction Read _____

Written By _____ Publication Date _____

I. Factual Summary: Write a short summary of the piece you read.

II. Vocabulary
    1. With which vocabulary words in the piece did you encounter some degree of difficulty?

    2. How did you resolve your lack of understanding with these words?

III. Interpretation: What was the main point the author wanted you to get from reading his work?

IV. Criticism
    1. With which points of the piece did you agree or find easy to accept? Why?

    2. With which points of the piece did you disagree or find difficult to believe? Why?

V. Personal Response: What do you think about this piece? <u>OR</u> How does this piece influence your ideas?

LESSON TWO

<u>Objectives</u>

    1. To read chapters 1-2

    2. To give students practice reading orally

    3. To evaluate students' oral reading

<u>Activity</u>

Have students read chapters 1-3 of *The Outsiders* out loud in class. You probably know the best way to get readers with your class; pick students at random, ask for volunteers, or use whatever method works best for your group. If you have not yet completed an oral reading evaluation for your students this marking period, this would be a good opportunity to do so. A form is included with this unit for your convenience.

If students do not complete reading chapters 1-2 in class, they should do so prior to your next class meeting.

ORAL READING EVALUATION - *The Outsiders*

Name _____ Class____ Date _____

SKILL	EXCELLENT	GOOD	AVERAGE	FAIR	POOR
Fluency	5	4	3	2	1
Clarity	5	4	3	2	1
Audibility	5	4	3	2	1
Pronunciation	5	4	3	2	1
_____	5	4	3	2	1
_____	5	4	3	2	1

Total _____   Grade _____

Comments:

LESSON THREE

Objectives

      1. To review the main events and ideas from chapters 1-2

      2. To preview the study questions for chapters 3-4

      3. To familiarize students with the vocabulary in chapters 3-4

      4. To read chapters 3-4

Activity #1

      Give students a few minutes to formulate answers for the study guide questions for chapters 1-2, and then discuss the answers to the questions in detail. Write the answers on the board or overhead transparency so students can have the correct answers for study purposes.

      NOTE: It is a good practice in public speaking and leadership skills for individual students to take charge of leading the discussions of the study questions. Perhaps a different student could go to the front of the class and lead the discussion each day that the study questions are discussed during this unit. Of course, the teacher should guide the discussion when appropriate and be sure to fill in any gaps the students leave.

Activity #2

      Give students about fifteen minutes to preview the study questions for chapters 3-4 of *The Outsiders* and to do the related vocabulary work.

Activity #3

      Continue the oral reading evaluations while choosing students to read chapters 3-4 orally in class. If students do not complete this assignment in class, they should complete it prior to your next class meeting.

LESSON FOUR

Objectives

     1. To check to see that students read chapters 3-4 as assigned

     2. To review the main ideas and events from chapters 3-4

     3. To preview the study questions for chapters 5-6

     4. To familiarize students with the vocabulary in chapters 5-6

     5. To read chapters 5-6

     6. To evaluate students' oral reading

Activity #1

     Quiz - Distribute quizzes for chapters 3-4 and give students about 10 minutes to complete them.

     NOTE: The quizzes may either be the short answer study guides or the multiple choice version. Have students exchange papers. Grade the quizzes as a class. Collect the papers for recording the grades. (If you used the multiple choice version as a quiz, take a few minutes to discuss the answers for the short answer version if your students are using the short answer version for their study guides.)

Activity #2

     Give students about 15 minutes to preview the study questions for chapters 5-6 and to do the related vocabulary work.

Activity #3

     Have students read chapters 5-6 orally for the remainder of the class period. Continue the oral reading evaluations. If students do not complete reading these chapters during this class period, they should do so prior to your next class meeting.

LESSON FIVE

Objectives

1. To have students complete a project in real life which is related to the fiction they are reading in class
2. To have students look at their own neighborhoods and consider the positive and negative influences there
3. To show students that they can have an impact in their own neighborhoods if they decide upon a good plan for making improvements

Activity

Group your students according to their neighborhoods; put students who live in the same neighborhoods together in groups.

Explain to students that there is a project that goes along with this *Outsiders* unit. In their neighborhood groups, students will first brainstorm a list of the positive and negative things that are in their neighborhoods. Next, they will decide which of the negative things they, as a Neighborhood Improvement Committee, would most like to make better. Students will make a plan of attack as to how they could improve the things they want to improve, giving each student in the group specific responsibilities, specific tasks to perform. Students will then carry out their plans of attack. This will probably require additional meeting time and time outside of school for completion.

Give each group a Neighborhood Improvement Committee Worksheet. Tell students that these worksheets are to help them get started and organize their committees' plans.

Give students the remainder of the class to meet and begin to make their plans. Explain that these projects are to be completed, if at all possible, by Lesson Sixteen (give students a day and date). That will allow them approximately 10-14 days to complete the project.

NEIGHBORHOOD IMPROVEMENT COMMITTEE WORKSHEET

1. Where is your neighborhood?

2. List here the names of the members of your committee.

1.

2.

3.

4.

5.

6.

7.

3. What are the best things your neighborhood has to offer?

4. What are the worst elements of your neighborhood?

5. Place a * next to the things in #4 you think you would most like to change about your neighborhood.

6. Circle the item(s) in #4 you think you could have the best chances of improving.

7. Describe in detail a plan--ways in which you could improve the item(s) you have circled in #4.

8. Next to each group member's name in #2 write in the specific tasks each person is to complete.

9. Will you meet again? When and where? For what purpose?

10. What shall be done prior to your next meeting?

11. Do you need special permission to do any of the things you plan to do? From whom do you get permission? How? (You should check with your teacher about this.)

12. What problems could you run into as a result of your activities?

13. How will you deal with those problems?

14. Does any group member have additional comments or suggestions? Note them here:

LESSON SIX

Objectives
1. To review the main ideas of chapters 5-6
2. To preview the study questions for chapters 7-9
3. To read chapters 7-9

Activity #1

Ask students to get out their books and some paper (not their study guides). Tell students to write down ten questions (and answers) which cover the main events and ideas in chapters 5-6.

Discuss the students questions and answers orally, making a list of the questions with brief responses on the board. Put a star next to the students' questions and answers that are essentially the same as the study guide questions. (Be sure that all the study guide questions are answered.)

Activity #2

Tell students to preview the study questions and do the vocabulary work for chapters 7-9.

Activity #3

Tell students that they should read chapters 7-9 prior to your next class meeting. If they have time after completing Activity #2, they may use the remainder of this class period to begin their reading.

LESSON SEVEN

Objectives
1. To review the main events of chapters 7-9
2. To check to see that students did the reading assignment
3. To assign the pre-reading, vocabulary and reading work for chapters 10-12

Activity #1

Give students a quiz on chapters 7-9. Use either the short answer or multiple choice form of the study guide questions as a quiz so that in discussing the answers to the quiz you also answer the study guide questions. Collect the papers for grade recording.

Activity #2

Tell students that prior to their next class period they must have completed the pre-reading, vocabulary and reading work for chapters 10-12. Students may have the remainder of this period to work on this assignment.

LESSON EIGHT

Objectives

    1. To review the main ideas and events from chapters 10-12

    2. To start students' thinking about their own lives in relation to the book

    3. To give students the opportunity to practice writing about themselves

    4. To give teachers the opportunity to evaluate students' writing

Activity #1

    Discuss the answers to the study guide questions for chapters 10-12 as you have done the other study questions.

Activity #2

    Distribute Writing Assignment #1. Explain the directions in detail, and then allow students ample time to complete the assignment.

Activity #3

    Collect the papers at the end of the period or at the beginning of the next period.

    Follow - Up: After you have graded the assignments, allow students to revise their papers using your suggestions and corrections. Give them about three days from the date they receive their papers to complete the revision. I suggest grading the revisions on an A-C-E scale (all revisions well-done, some revisions made, few or no revisions made). This will speed your grading time and still give some credit for the students' efforts.

WRITING ASSIGNMENT #1 - *The Outsiders*

PROMPT

As Pony says, "Things are rough all over. . . ." Everyone, no matter whether a Greaser or a Soc or any other gang or group, has some sort of conflict in life. That's just the nature of things, people being human.

Your assignment is the same as Pony's was: Write a theme about "anything you think is important enough to write about. And it isn't a reference theme; I want your own ideas and experiences."

PREWRITING

One way to begin is to think about the conflict(s) in your own life. Writing about something that is already on your mind is sometimes easier than thinking about an "issue." Is there something that really bugs you? Something you have to deal with (and would rather not)? What is it? How can the conflict be resolved? What do you think is the best solution?

If you choose, you may write about an issue in your community or an issue which relates to all people; anything you think is worth writing about is fair game.

Your theme should be at least 500 words long; no longer than about 1000 words. If you feel it needs to be longer than that, get special permission.

DRAFTING

Begin with an introductory paragraph in which you introduce the topic about which you are writing.

Follow that with a logical progression of ideas in which you describe the problem or issue and give your opinions about the issue or problem.

Finish with a paragraph giving your conclusions related to the problem or issue.

PROMPT

When you finish the rough draft of your paper, ask a student who sits near you to read it. After reading your rough draft, he/she should tell you what he/she liked best about your work, which parts were difficult to understand, and ways in which your work could be improved. Reread your paper considering your critic's comments, and make the corrections you think are necessary.

PROOFREADING

Do a final proofreading of your paper double-checking your grammar, spelling, organization, and the clarity of your ideas.

LESSONS NINE AND TEN

Objectives
   1. To prepare students to discuss *The Outsiders* on interpretive and critical levels
   2. To begin discussing *The Outsiders* on interpretive and critical levels

Activity #1
   Choose the questions from the Extra Discussion Questions/Writing Assignments which seem most appropriate for your students. A class discussion of these questions is most effective if students have been given the opportunity to formulate answers to the questions prior to the discussion. To this end, you may either have all the students formulate answers to all the questions, divide your class into groups and assign one or more questions to each group, or you could assign one question to each student in your class. The option you choose will make a difference in the amount of class time needed for this activity. Two class periods are allotted assuming you will cover most of the questions offered. If you need less time, skip to Lesson Eleven.

Activity #3
   After students have had ample time to formulate answers to the questions, begin your class discussion of the questions and the ideas presented by the questions. Be sure students take notes during the discussion so they have information to study for the unit test.

EXTRA WRITING ASSIGNMENTS AND/OR DISCUSSION QUESTIONS - *The Outsiders*

Interpretation

1. Where is the climax of the story?
2. The members of Pony's gang are all individuals. Give character sketches of Ponyboy, Johnny, Soda, Darry, Dallas, Two-Bit and Steve.
3. Explain the importance of the setting in *The Outsiders*.
4. In what ways does Ms. Hinton attempt to make the story believable? Is he successful?
5. What is the difference between a "hood" and a "greaser"?
6. Why do Greasers and Socs fight?
7. Discuss the importance of the fire in the development of the theme. (Suppose there had been no fire. How would the book have changed?)
8. At what times and how were the barriers between Greasers and Socs broken?

Critical

9. Ponyboy's perception of Darry changes in the course of the story. Explain how.
10. Compare and contrast Dally and Bob.
11. Explain how the title of the book is appropriate.
12. What is the symbolic importance of each of the following: Dally's jacket, the church, Pony's haircut, sunset, sunrise, and Pepsi-Cola.
13. Evaluate S. E. Hinton's style of writing. How does it contribute to the value of the novel?
14. Explain the meaning of Frost's poem as it relates to *The Outsiders*.
15. How does *Gone With the Wind* relate to *The Outsiders*?
16. Pony passes through several stages in the book. Define the stages he passes through as his character develops. Use examples from the text.
17. What faults in our society does S. E. Hinton point out in *The Outsiders*?
18. Compare and contrast the boys who died: Bob, Dally and Johnny.
19. Compare and contrast the circumstances of the boys' deaths and explain the significance.
20. Compare and contrast Johnny and Ponyboy.
21. Is Ponyboy still "gold" at the end of the story? Explain your answer.
22. Was Dally a hood or a greaser?
23. Is *The Outsiders* a tragedy? If so, how? If not, why not?

Critical/Personal Response

24. If you were to rewrite *The Outsiders* as a play, where would you start and end each act?
25. Choose another title for the book and explain your choice.
26. Cherry felt that the whole mess was her fault. Was it?

27. Who is responsible for Bob's death? Johnny's? Dally's?
28. Suppose the story had ended in the parking lot at the grocery store, with Ponyboy's repeating Dally's words, ". . . Get smart and nothing can touch you. . . ." How would that have changed the message of the book?
29. What were we supposed to learn from reading *The Outsiders*?

Personal Response
30. Did you enjoy reading *The Outsiders*? Why or why not?
31. Define "hero."
32. Define "gallant."
33. Did the fact that Bob and his friends were drunk excuse their behavior?

LESSON ELEVEN

Objective

To review all of the vocabulary work done in this unit

Activity

Choose one (or more) of the vocabulary review activities listed on the next page(s) and spend your class period as directed in the activity. Some of the materials for these review activities are located in the Extra Activities section in this unit.

VOCABULARY REVIEW ACTIVITIES

1. Divide your class into two teams and have an old-fashioned spelling or definition bee.

2. Give each of your students (or students in groups of two, three or four) a *The Outsiders* Vocabulary Word Search Puzzle. The person (group) to find all of the vocabulary words in the puzzle first wins.

3. Give students a *The Outsiders* Vocabulary Word Search Puzzle without the word list. The person or group to find the most vocabulary words in the puzzle wins.

4. Use a *The Outsiders* Vocabulary Crossword Puzzle. Put the puzzle onto a transparency on the overhead projector (so everyone can see it), and do the puzzle together as a class.

5. Give students a *The Outsiders* Vocabulary Matching Worksheet to do.

6. Divide your class into two teams. Use the *Outsiders* vocabulary words with their letters jumbled as a word list. Student 1 from Team A faces off against Student 1 from Team B. You write the first jumbled word on the board. The first student (1A or 1B) to unscramble the word wins the chance for his/her team to score points. If 1A wins the jumble, go to student 2A and give him/her a definition. He/she must give you the correct spelling of the vocabulary word which fits that definition. If he/she does, Team A scores a point, and you give student 3A a definition for which you expect a correctly spelled matching vocabulary word. Continue giving Team A definitions until some team member makes an incorrect response. An incorrect response sends the game back to the jumbled-word face off, this time with students 2A and 2B. Instead of repeating giving definitions to the first few students of each team, continue with the student after the one who gave the last incorrect response on the team. For example, if Team B wins the jumbled-word face-off, and student 5B gave the last incorrect answer for Team B, you would start this round of definition questions with student 6B, and so on. The team with the most points wins!

7. Have students write a story in which they correctly use as many vocabulary words as possible. Have students read their compositions orally! Post the most original compositions on your bulletin board.

LESSON TWELVE

Objectives

    1. To review and reinforce the main ideas and events of the story

    2. To consider the significance of several of the quotations from the story

    3. To take a closer look at the importance of the language selected in writing the story

    4. To give students time to work on their nonfiction reading assignments

Activity #1

    Distribute the Quotations Worksheet. Discuss the significance or importance of each quote listed.

Activity #2

    If time remains at after completing activity 1, give students time to work on their nonfiction reading assignments. You will probably already have nonfiction materials available for students to read in your in-class library related to this unit.

QUOTATIONS WORKSHEET - *The Outsiders*

1. Darry's gone through a lot in his twenty years, grown up too fast. Sodapop'll never grow up at all. I don't know which way's the best. I'll find out one of these days. (1)

2. He [Dally] started to put his arm around her, but Johnny reached over and stopped him. (2)

3. You've seen too much to be innocent. (Cherry to Pony, Ch 2)

4. I really couldn't see what Socs would have to sweat about -- good grades, good cars, good girls, madras and Mustangs and Corvairs -- Man, I thought, if I had worries like that I'd consider myself lucky. I know better now. (2)

5. She was coming through to me all right, probably because I was a Greaser, and younger; she didn't have to keep her guard up with me. (3)

6. We're always going and going and going, and never asking where. (3)

7. We saw the same sunset. (3)

8. "Shut up talkin' like that," Two-Bit said fiercely, messing up Johnny's hair. "We couldn't get along without you, so you can just shut up!" (3)

9. Ponyboy . . . I mean . . . if I see you in the hall at school or someplace and don't say hi, well, it's not personal or anything, but . . . (3)

10. I could fall in love with Dallas Winston. I hope I never see him again, or I will. (3)

11. I just couldn't take it or leave it, like Two-Bit, or ignore it and love life anyway, like Sodapop, or harden myself beyond caring, like Dally, or actually enjoy it, like Tim Shepard. (3)

12. It seems there's gotta be someplace without Greasers or Socs, with just people. Plain ordinary people. (3)

13. Our hair labeled us Greasers, too -- it was our trademark. The one thing we were proud of. Maybe we couldn't have Corvairs or madras shirts, but we could have hair. (5)

14. We're all cried out now. We're gettin' used to the idea. We're gonna be okay now. (5)

15. He [Johnny] was especially stuck on the Southern gentlemen -- impressed with their manners and charm. (5)

16. Dally was real. I liked my books and clouds and sunsets. Dally was so real he scared me. (5)

17. "Dally!" I said, frightened. "You kill people with heaters!"
    "Ya kill 'em with switchblades, too, don't ya, kid?" (5)

18. She [Cherry] said she felt that the whole mess was her fault, which it is, . . . (6)

19. No, it wasn't Cherry the Soc who was helping us, it was Cherry the dreamer who watched sunsets and couldn't stand fights. (6)

20. My parents, did they ask about me? (Johnny, Ch 6)

21. Oh, blast it, Johnny . . . you get hardened in jail. I don't want that to happen to you. Like it happened to me . . . (6)

22. That jacket saved you from a bad burning, maybe saved your life. (6)

23. I had taken the long way around, but I was finally home. To stay. (6)

24. Asleep, he looked a lot younger than going-on-seventeen, but I had noticed that Johnny looked younger when he was asleep, too, so I figured everyone did. Maybe people are younger when they are asleep. (7)

25. What I like is the 'turn' bit. Y'all were heroes from the beginning. You just didn't 'turn' all of a sudden. (7)

26. What's the safest thing to be when one is met by a gang of social outcasts in an alley? . . . another social outcast! (7)

27. You can't win, even if you whip us. You'll still be where you were before -- at the bottom. And we'll still be the lucky ones with all the breaks. (7)

28. My name is Ponyboy. Nice talkin' to you, Randy. (8)

29. We needed Johnny as much as he needed the gang. And for the same reason. (8)

30. I hoped the nurse would have enough sense not to let Johnny's mother see him. It would kill him. (8)

31. You'd think you could get away with murder, living with your big brother and all, but Darry's stricter than your folks were, ain't he? (8)

32. Darry was too smart to be a Greaser. I don't know how I knew, I just did. And I was kind of sorry. (8)

33. He [Two-Bit] seemed to feel that if you said something was all right, it immediately was, no matter what. (8)

34. Why do people sell liquor to boys? Why? I know there's a law against it, but kids get it anyway. (8)

35. You're a traitor to your own kind and not loyal to us. (8)

36. What kind of a world is it where all I have to be proud of is a reputation for being a hood, and greasy hair? (9)

37. Nobody ever gets really hurt in a skin rumble. (9)

38. I knew Darry as well as he knew me, and that isn't saying a whole lot. (9)

39. We're Greasers, but not hoods, and we don't belong with this bunch of future convicts. (9)

40. -- half of the hoods I know are pretty decent guys underneath all that grease, and from what I've heard, a lot of Socs are just cold-blooded mean -- but people usually go by looks. (9)

41. That's stupid, I thought swiftly, they've both come here to fight and they're both supposed to be smarter than that. What difference does the side make? (9)

42. They used to be buddies, I thought, they used to be friends, and now they hate each other because one has to work for a living and the other comes from the West Side. They shouldn't hate each other . . . I don't hate the Socs any more . . . (9)

43. Two friends of mine had died that night: one a hero, the other a hoodlum. (10)

44. Nothing we can do . . . not for Dally or Johnny or Tim Shepard or any of us . . . . (10)

45. Is Darry sorry I'm sick? (10)

46. I'd never get past the part where the Southern gentlemen go riding into sure death because they are gallant. (10)

47. It used to be that I'd just stand there and let Darry yell at me, but lately I'd been yelling right back. (12)

48. Remembering a handsome, dark boy with a reckless grin and a hot temper. A tough, towheaded boy with a cigarette in his mouth and a bitter grin on his hard face. Remembering -- and this time it didn't hurt -- a quiet, defeated-looking sixteen-year-old whose hair needed cutting badly and who had black eyes with a frightened expression to them. One week had taken all three of them. (12)

LESSONS THIRTEEN AND FOURTEEN

Objectives
1. To evaluate students' writing
2. To have students revise their writing assignment 1 papers
3. To show students the film *The Outsiders* in preparation for writing assignment 3

NOTE: YOU NEED TO GO TO YOUR LOCAL VIDEO STORE PRIOR TO THIS LESSON TO RENT A COPY OF <u>THE OUTSIDERS</u>.

Activity #1

Show the film *The Outsiders* to your class, asking them to make mental notes about how the characters, scenery, and action may be different from how they were in the book and how they imagined them to be as they read the book.

Activity #2

While students are watching the movie, call individual students to your desk (or some other private area) to discuss their papers from Writing Assignment 1. A Writing Evaluation Form is included with this unit to help structure your conferences.

LESSON FIFTEEN

Objectives
1. To give students the opportunity to practice writing to persuade
2. To give students the chance to critically analyze the film and book of *The Outsiders*
3. To give the teacher a chance to evaluate students' individual writing
4. To give students the opportunity to correct their writing errors and produce an error-free paper

Activity #1

Distribute Writing Assignment #2. Discuss the directions orally in detail. Allow the remaining class time for students to complete the activity.

If students do not have enough class time to finish, the papers may be collected at the beginning of the next class period.

Follow-Up: Follow up as in Writing Assignment 1, allowing students to correct their errors and turn in the revision for credit. A good time for your next writing conferences would be the day following the unit test.

WRITING EVALUATION FORM - *The Outsiders*

Name _____ Date _____

Writing Assignment #1 for the *Outsiders* unit   Grade _____

Circle One For Each Item:

Letter Format: correct   errors noted on paper

Character Analysis: excellent   good   fair   poor

Grammar: correct   errors noted on paper

Spelling: correct   errors noted on paper

Punctuation: correct   errors noted on paper

Legibility: excellent   good   fair   poor

Strengths:

Weaknesses:

Comments/Suggestions:

WRITING ASSIGNMENT #2 - *The Outsiders*

PROMPT

You have read the book *The Outsiders* and you have seen a film of the story, too. You have a friend who equally loves to read and to watch movies, and she is trying to decide whether to read the book or watch the movie. Your job is to persuade her to either read the book OR to watch the movie based on your critical analysis of them both.

PREWRITING

One way to start is to make a list of similarities and differences between the book and the film. Make a list of the main characters. Were they portrayed the same in the book as in the movie? Was the plot exactly the same in the movie as in the book? In what ways was the movie different from the book? Which did you like better: the film or the book? Why? Based on these observations, decide which you would recommend to your friend.

DRAFTING

Write an introductory paragraph in which you let your friend know that you are aware of her predicament in deciding whether to read the book or see the film for *The Outsiders* and to let her know that you have done both.

The paragraphs which follow should give your reasons for choosing the book over the film or the film over the book. You could allow one paragraph for each reason, fully explaining each with examples from the text and/or film.

The final paragraph should be the ultimate conclusion the paragraphs above have hinted towards.

PROMPT

When you finish the rough draft of your paper, ask a student who sits near you to read it. After reading your rough draft, he/she should tell you what he/she liked best about your work, which parts were difficult to understand, and ways in which your work could be improved. Reread your paper considering your critic's comments, and make the corrections you think are necessary.

PROOFREADING

Do a final proofreading of your paper double-checking your grammar, spelling, organization, and the clarity of your ideas.

LESSON SIXTEEN

Objectives

1. To give students the opportunity to practice public speaking
2. To have students share the experiences they have had doing their group projects
3. To draw the group projects to a conclusion
4. To have students practice writing to inform
5. To give the teacher the chance to evaluate students' writing and the group projects

Activity #1

Give students about ten minutes to meet in their groups to discuss any last-minute, final tidbits they may want or need to exchange and to recap their whole project together.

Activity #2

Call forward one spokesperson from each group to give a summary of that group's activities for the duration of the project.

Activity #3

Distribute Writing Assignment 3. Discuss the directions in detail and give students the remainder of this class period to work on the assignment.

Note: Students may need more time than just the remainder of the class period to complete this assignment. Consider the level of your class and give students a day and a date when the writing assignments will be due.

PROMPT

You have spent time in your Neighborhood Improvement Committee trying to improve your neighborhood. Now it is time to stop and think about what you have done and to evaluate your success.

Your assignment is to write a written report summarizing your group's efforts and evaluating the impact your group had on your neighborhood.

PREWRITING

Jot down notes answering each of the following questions:

Where is your neighborhood?

What improvement(s) did your group attempt to make in your neighborhood?

How did you attempt to make those improvements? What was your plan?

Did you encounter any problems with your plan? If so, how were they resolved?

Was your plan successful? Did you accomplish all that you had hoped to accomplish?

Is there anything you could have done differently to have made your plan more successful? (Knowing what you know now, would you have done anything differently?)

How do you feel about what you and your group members did in your neighborhood? What are your own thoughts about your project?

DRAFTING

Write one "section" in your report answering each of the above questions.
Location , Improvements Planned, The Plan, Problems,
Evaluation, A Better Plan, My Own Conclusions

PROMPT

When you finish the rough draft of your paper, ask a student who sits near you to read it. After reading your rough draft, he/she should tell you what he/she liked best about your work, which parts were difficult to understand, and ways in which your work could be improved. Reread your paper considering your critic's comments, and make the corrections you think are necessary.

PROOFREADING

Do a final proofreading of your paper double-checking your grammar, spelling, organization, and the clarity of your ideas.

LESSON SEVENTEEN

Objectives

       1. To widen the breadth of students' knowledge about the topics discussed or
         touched upon in *The Outsiders*
       2. To check students' nonfiction reading assignments

Activity

      Ask each student to give a brief oral report about the nonfiction work he/she read for the nonfiction reading assignment. Your criteria for evaluating this report will vary depending on the level of your students. You may wish for students to give a complete report without using notes of any kind, or you may want students to read directly from a written report, or you may want to do something in between these two extremes. Just make students aware of your criteria in ample time for them to prepare their reports.

      Start with one student's report. After that, ask if anyone else in the class has read on a topic related to the first student's report. If no one has, choose another student at random. After each report, be sure to ask if anyone has a report related to the one just completed. That will help keep a continuity during the discussion of the reports.

LESSON EIGHTEEN

Objectives
1. To have students take their knowledge of all of the major elements of *The Outsiders* beyond the pages of the book
2. To give students the opportunity to express their personal opinions and use their creativity
3. To have students work together as a group for a common purpose
4. To have students practice evaluating suggestions, choosing the best suggestions, and compromising when necessary

Activity

The teacher will lead the class in a group writing activity. The whole class will participate in writing a plot summary of *The Outsiders II*.

Students should decide on how much time has passed since "*The Outsiders I*" has taken place. One way to then tackle the writing assignment is for students to decide what would logically happen to each character in the sequel. After you do a character or two, you will probably find the characters interacting with each other (what one does affects another). If your students aren't inclined to "jump in and run" with this assignment, start by asking specific students specific questions. For example, Student A, what do you think Pony would do in the sequel? Student B, do you agree with Student A, or do you think Pony would do something different? Jot down the events upon which your students decide, and use that as a rough draft from which to write. Have students give you specific sentences to write in your plot summary. Review and revise the summary as a class until you have a good, finished product.

If you wish to take this writing assignment one step further, you could then assign roles to various students in your class and have them create the dialogue for each scene by improvising and interacting as their characters. Making and viewing a video tape of this activity is fun and constructive.

LESSON NINETEEN

Objective

To review the main ideas presented in *The Outsiders*

Activity #1

Choose one of the review games/activities included in the packet and spend your class period as outlined there. Some materials for these activities are located in the Extra Activities Packet section of this unit.

Activity #2

Remind students that the Unit Test will be in the next class meeting. Stress the review of the Study Guides and their class notes as a last minute, brush-up review for homework.

REVIEW GAMES/ACTIVITIES - *The Outsiders*

1. Ask the class to make up a unit test for *The Outsiders*. The test should have 4 sections: matching, true/false, short answer, and essay. Students may use 1/2 period to make the test and then swap papers and use the other 1/2 class period to take a test a classmate has devised. (open book) You may want to use the unit test included in this packet or take questions from the students' unit tests to formulate your own test.

2. Take 1/2 period for students to make up true and false questions (including the answers). Collect the papers and divide the class into two teams. Draw a big tic-tac-toe board on the chalk board. Make one team X and one team O. Ask questions to each side, giving each student one turn. If the question is answered correctly, that students' team's letter (X or O) is placed in the box. If the answer is incorrect, no mark is placed in the box. The object is to get three marks in a row like tic-tac-toe. You may want to keep track of the number of games won for each team.

3. Take 1/2 period for students to make up questions (true/false and short answer). Collect the questions. Divide the class into two teams. You'll alternate asking questions to individual members of teams A & B (like in a spelling bee). The question keeps going from A to B until it is correctly answered, then a new question is asked. A correct answer does not allow the team to get another question. Correct answers are +2 points; incorrect answers are -1 point.

4. Have students pair up and quiz each other from their study guides and class notes.

5. Give students a *The Outsiders* crossword puzzle to complete.

6. Divide your class into two teams. Use the *Outsiders* crossword words with their letters jumbled as a word list. Student 1 from Team A faces off against Student 1 from Team B. You write the first jumbled word on the board. The first student (1A or 1B) to unscramble the word wins the chance for his/her team to score points. If 1A wins the jumble, go to student 2A and give him/her a clue. He/she must give you the correct word which matches that clue. If he/she does, Team A scores a point, and you give student 3A a clue for which you expect another correct response. Continue giving Team A clues until some team member makes an incorrect response. An incorrect response sends the game back to the jumbled-word face off, this time with students 2A and 2B. Instead of repeating giving clues to the first few students of each team, continue with the student after the one who gave the last incorrect response on the team. For example, if Team B wins the jumbled-word face-off, and student 5B gave the last incorrect answer for Team B, you would start this round of clue questions with student 6B, and so on. The team with the most points wins!

UNIT TESTS

SHORT ANSWER UNIT TEST 1 - *The Outsiders*

I. Short Answer

1. How are Greasers different from Socs?

2. Contrast Dally's approach to Cherry and Marcia with Pony's, and contrast Cherry's response to Dally with her response to Pony.

3. After talking with Cherry, what reason does Pony give for the separation between Greasers and Socs?

4. Why was Pony upset about getting a haircut?

5. Describe Johnny's relationship with his parents. Describe his relationship with Dally.

6. For what reasons did Darry, Steve, Soda and Two-Bit fight?

7. What advice did Dally give to Pony on the way to the hospital after the rumble?

8. What were Johnny's last words to Pony?

9. How did Pony react to the Socs who bullied him about killing Bob?

10. Johnny's note made several points. What were they?

II. Quotes: Explain the significance of 15 of the following quotations.

1. Darry's gone through a lot in his twenty years, grown up too fast. Sodapop'll never grow up at all. I don't know which way's the best. I'll find out one of these days.

2. I really couldn't see what Socs would have to sweat about -- good grades, good cars, good girls, madras and Mustangs and Corvairs -- Man, I thought, if I had worries like that I'd consider myself lucky. I know better now.

3. We saw the same sunset.

4. It seems like there's gotta be someplace without Greasers or Socs, with just people. Plain ordinary people.

5. My parents, did they ask about me?

6. Oh, blast it, Johnny, you get hardened in jail. I don't want that to happen to you. Like it happened to me.

7. That jacket saved you from a bad burning, maybe saved your life.

8. Asleep, he looked a lot younger than going-on-seventeen, but I had noticed that Johnny looked younger when he was asleep, too, so I figured everyone did. Maybe people are younger when they are asleep.

9. Y'all were heroes from the beginning. You just didn't 'turn' all of a sudden.

10. My name's Ponyboy. Nice talkin' to you, Randy.

11. You're a traitor to your own kind and not loyal to us.

12. What kind of a world is it where all I have to be proud of is a reputation for being a hood, and greasy hair?

13. That's stupid, I thought swiftly, they've both come to fight and they're both supposed to be smarter than that. What difference does the side make?

14. Stay gold, Ponyboy. Stay gold. . .

15. You get back into your car or you'll get split.

16. I had the knife. I killed Bob.

17. Two friends of mine died that night: one a hero, the other a hoodlum.

III. Vocabulary

Listen to the words given. Write them down. Go back later and write in the definitions.

1.

2.

3.

4.

5.

6.

7.

8.

9.

10.

SHORT ANSWER UNIT TEST 2 - *The Outsiders*

I. Short Answer
1. Identify Darry, Soda and Ponyboy.

2. How are Greasers different from Socs?

3. Contrast Dally's approach to Cherry and Marcia with Pony's, and contrast Cherry's response to Dally with her response to Pony.

4. What happened to Johnny and Ponyboy at the park?

5. Describe Johnny's relationship with his parents.

6. What happened when Johnny, Pony and Dally returned to the church?

7. Compare and contrast the boys' reasons for fighting. (Darry, Steve, Soda and Two-Bit)

8. What advice did Dally give to Pony on the way to the hospital after the rumble?

9. What did Pony decide was the reason Dally couldn't take Johnny's death?

10. Johnny's note made several points. What were they?

KEY: SHORT ANSWER UNIT TESTS - *The Outsiders*

The short answer questions are taken directly from the study guides.
If you need to look up the answers, you will find them in the study guide section.

Answers to the composition questions will vary depending on your
class discussions and the level of your students.

For the vocabulary section of the test, choose ten of the
words from the vocabulary lists to read orally for your students.

ADVANCED SHORT ANSWER UNIT TEST - *The Outsiders*

I. Short Answer

1. Ponyboy's perception of Darry changes in the course of the story. Explain how.

2. Pony passes through several stages in the book. Define the stages he passes through as his character develops. Use examples from the text.

3. Compare and contrast the boys who died and the circumstances of their deaths.

4. Compare and contrast Johnny and Ponyboy.

5. Is *The Outsiders* a tragedy? If so, how? If not, why not?

II. Quotations Explain the significance or importance of each of the following quotations.

1. I really couldn't see what Socs would have to sweat about -- good grades, good cars, good girls, madras and Mustangs and Corvairs -- Man, I thought, if I had worries like that I'd consider myself lucky. I know better now. (2)

2. We saw the same sunset. (3)

3. Dally was real. I liked my books and clouds and sunsets. Dally was so real he scared me. (5)

4. She [Cherry] said she felt that the whole mess was her fault, which it is, . . . (6)

5. My parents, did they ask about me? (Johnny, Ch 6)

6. Asleep, he looked a lot younger than going-on-seventeen, but I had noticed that Johnny looked younger when he was asleep, too, so I figured everyone did. Maybe people are younger when they are asleep. (7)

7. What I like is the 'turn' bit. Y'all were heroes from the beginning. You just didn't 'turn' all of a sudden. (7)

8. My name is Ponyboy. Nice talkin' to you, Randy. (8)

9. Two friends of mine had died that night: one a hero, the other a hoodlum. (10)

10. Remembering a handsome, dark boy with a reckless grin and a hot temper. A tough, towheaded boy with a cigarette in his mouth and a bitter grin on his hard face. Remembering -- and this time it didn't hurt -- a quiet, defeated-looking sixteen-year-old whose hair needed cutting badly and who had black eyes with a frightened expression to them. One week had taken all three of them. (12)

III. Vocabulary

Listen to the vocabulary words and write them down. Then go back and write a composition relating in some way to *The Outsiders* using all of the words.

IV. Composition

One author from Horn Book wrote, "This remarkable novel gives a moving, credible view of the outsiders from the inside--their loyalty to each other, and their sensitivity under tough crusts, their understanding of self and society." Justify this comment using examples from the text.

MULTIPLE CHOICE UNIT TEST 1 - *The Outsiders*

I. Matching

1. Bob	A. Tried to call off the big rumble
2. Cherry	B. Author
3. Dallas	C. Police shot him
4. Darry	D. Middle brother
5. Hinton	E. The narrator
6. Johnny	F. Johnny killed him
7. Paul	G. Pony's eldest brother
8. Ponyboy	H. He killed Bob & saved the children
9. Randy	I. Holden; He started a rumble
10. Sodapop	J. Became a Greaser spy

II. Multiple Choice

1. After talking with Cherry, what reason does Pony finally give for the separation between Greasers and Socs?
   a. Feelings
   b. Education
   c. Money
   d. Background

2. Why was Pony late coming home from the Nightly Double?
   a. He and Johnny fell asleep at the movie
   b. He got into a fight
   c. They were busy talking to Cherry
   d. He and Johnny fell asleep looking at the stars

3. To whom do Johnny and Pony turn for help after Johnny killed Bob?
   a. Dally
   b. Darry
   c. Cherry
   d. Two-Bit

4. Why did Johnny and Pony go to Jay's Mountain?
   a. To hide out in the back woods
   b. To get across the state line
   c. To hide out at the church there
   d. To meet Two-Bit

5. Describe Johnny's relationship with his parents.
      a. His parents were a close loving family
      b. His parents ignored him and beat him up
      c. Johnny hated his parents but they loved him
      d. Johnny didn't care about his parents and they didn't care about him

6. What happened when Johnny, Pony and Dally returned to the church?
      a. The preacher found them
      b. The church had caught on fire
      c. They blew up the church
      d. The police had surrounded the building and were waiting for them

7. How do we know Dally felt at least partially responsible for Johnny's fate?
      a. He taught Johnny about the importance of being heroic
      b. He forced his ideas about putting others before yourself onto Johnny
      c. He kept Johnny from becoming "hard"
      d. None of the above

8. What advice did Dally give to Pony on the way to the hospital after the rumble?
      a. "Get tough like me and you won't get hurt."
      b. "Do unto other as you want them to do unto you."
      c. "Move away while you can."
      d. "Revenge is always best."

9. What did Pony decide was the reason Dally couldn't take Johnny's death?
      a. Dally made Johnny go back into the burning building and was therefore the cause of Johnny's death
      b. Dally couldn't deal with any death.
      c. Dally couldn't ever handle reality.
      d. Johnny was the only thing Dally loved.

10. Johnny's note made several points. Which one was <u>NOT</u> one of Johnny's points?
      a. There is still good in the world.
      b. He didn't mind dying for those kids.
      c. Pony can make whatever he wants of his life.
      d. He forgives his mother and father.

III. Vocabulary - Match the definitions to the appropriate words.

1. Elite

A. confusion, disordered speech, hallucinations

2. Veered

B. suddenly

3. Asset

C. selling alcohol where not legally available

4. Gorged

D. worth

5. Premonition

E. swerved, turned aside from a course or direction

6. Acquitted

F. to breathe into the lungs

7. Slouched

G. imitating, ridiculing

8. Delirious

H. discharged completely, set free from a legal charge

9. Rarely

I. scornful, insolent

10. Complicated

J. bitter cutting jest

11. Sarcasm

K. not fully awake

12. Deny

L. a select body, the best

13. Contemptuously

M. uncommon, infrequent

14. Inhalation

N. involved, complex

15. Nonchalantly

O. to declare untrue; contradict

16. Aimlessly

P. an ungainly gait

17. Bootlegging

Q. previous warning, information, feeling

18. Mimicking

R. without direction, without purpose

19. Abruptly

S. indifferently

20. Groggy

T. swallow with greediness

IV. Composition

One author from Horn Book wrote, "This remarkable novel gives a moving, credible view of the outsiders from the inside--their loyalty to each other, and their sensitivity under tough crusts, their understanding of self and society." Justify this comment using examples from the text.

MULTIPLE CHOICE UNIT TEST 2 - *The Outsiders*

I. Matching

1. Bob	A. Author
2. Cherry	B. Tried to call off the big rumble
3. Dallas	C. Pony's eldest brother
4. Darry	D. Became a Greaser spy
5. Hinton	E. He killed Bob & saved the children
6. Johnny	F. Johnny killed him
7. Paul	G. Police shot him
8. Ponyboy	H. The narrator
9. Randy	I. Holden; He started a rumble
10. Sodapop	J. Middle brother

II. Multiple Choice

1. After talking with Cherry, what reason does Pony finally give for the separation between Greasers and Socs?
   a. Background
   b. Education
   c. Money
   d. Feelings

2. Why was Pony late coming home from the Nightly Double?
   a. He and Johnny fell asleep at the movie
   b. He got into a fight
   c. He and Johnny fell asleep looking at the stars
   d. They were busy talking to Cherry

3. To whom do Johnny and Pony turn for help after Johnny killed Bob?
   a. Cherry
   b. Darry
   c. Dally
   d. Two-Bit

4. Why did Johnny and Pony go to Jay's Mountain?
   a. To hide out in the back woods
   b. To hide out at the church there
   c. To get across the state line
   d. To meet Two-Bit

5. Describe Johnny's relationship with his parents.
   a. His parents ignored him and beat him up
   b. His parents were a close loving family
   c. Johnny hated his parents but they loved him
   d. Johnny didn't care about his parents and they didn't care about him

6. What happened when Johnny, Pony and Dally returned to the church?
   a. The preacher found them
   b. They blew up the church
   c. The church had caught on fire
   d. The police had surrounded the building and were waiting for them

7. How do we know Dally felt at least partially responsible for Johnny's fate?
   a. He taught Johnny about the importance of being heroic
   b. He kept Johnny from becoming "hard"
   c. He forced his ideas about putting others before yourself onto Johnny
   d. None of the above

8. What advice did Dally give to Pony on the way to the hospital after the rumble?
   a. "Do unto other as you want them to do unto you."
   b. "Get tough like me and you won't get hurt."
   c. "Move away while you can."
   d. "Revenge is always best."

9. What did Pony decide was the reason Dally couldn't take Johnny's death?
   a. Johnny was the only thing Dally loved.
   b. Dally couldn't ever handle reality.
   c. Dally couldn't deal with any death.
   d. Dally made Johnny go back into the burning building and was therefore the cause of Johnny's death

10. Johnny's note made several points. Which one was <u>NOT</u> one of Johnny's points?
    a. There is still good in the world.
    b. He didn't mind dying for those kids.
    c. Pony can make whatever he wants of his life.
    d. He forgives his mother and father.

III. Vocabulary - Match the definitions to the appropriate words.

1. Sullenly   a. afraid, suspicious

2. Bewildering   b. confusion, disordered speech, hallucinations

3. Madras   c. involved, complex

4. Vital   d. confused, perplexed

5. Apprehensive   e. cotton fabric shirt usually brightly colored

6. Quivering   f. to breathe into the lungs

7. Groggy   g. cultured, worldly

8. Inhalation   h. heroic acts, adventures

9. Reluctantly   i. compassion for suffering

10. Exploits   j. essential, necessary to life

11. Cowlick   k. trembling, shaking

12. Incredulous   l. unbelieving

13. Bootlegging   m. senses are deadened

14. Complicated   n. unwillingly, struggling

15. Pity   o. escaped, avoided

16. Delirious   p. selling alcohol where not legally available

17. Sophisticated   q. gloomily, somber

18. Eluded   r. not fully awake

19. Sarcasm   s. bitter cutting jest

20. Stupor   t. tuft of hair growing in a different direction

III. Composition

Write a composition in which you choose one word to describe the book *The Outsiders* and defend your choice using examples from the text. (ie. hopeful, depressing, realistic, or any other descriptive word of your choice)

ANSWER SHEET:- MULTIPLE CHOICE TESTS - *The Outsiders*

I. Matching	II. Multiple Choice	III. Vocabulary
1. ____	1. (A) (B) (C) (D)	1. ____
2. ____	2. (A) (B) (C) (D)	2. ____
3. ____	3. (A) (B) (C) (D)	3. ____
4. ____	4. (A) (B) (C) (D)	4. ____
5. ____	5. (A) (B) (C) (D)	5. ____
6. ____	6. (A) (B) (C) (D)	6. ____
7. ____	7. (A) (B) (C) (D)	7. ____
8. ____	8. (A) (B) (C) (D)	8. ____
9. ____	9. (A) (B) (C) (D)	9. ____
10. ____	10. (A) (B) (C) (D)	10. ____
		11. ____
		12. ____
		13. ____
		14. ____
		15. ____
		16. ____
		17. ____
		18. ____
		19. ____
		20. ____

ANSWER KEY - MULTIPLE CHOICE TEST 1
The Outsiders

I. Matching

1.   F
2.   J
3.   C
4.   G
5.   B
6.   H
7.   I
8.   E
9.   A
10.   D

II. Multiple Choice

1. ( ) (B) (C) (D)
2. (A) (B) (C) ( )
3. ( ) (B) (C) (D)
4. (A) (B) ( ) (D)
5. (A) ( ) (C) (D)
6. (A) ( ) (C) (D)
7. (A) (B) ( ) (D)
8. ( ) (B) (C) (D)
9. (A) (B) (C) ( )
10. (A) (B) (C) ( )

III. Vocabulary

1.   L
2.   E
3.   D
4.   T
5.   Q
6.   H
7.   P
8.   A
9.   M
10.   N
11.   J
12.   O
13.   I
14.   F
15.   S
16.   R
17.   C
18.   G
19.   B
20.   K

ANSWER KEY- MULTIPLE CHOICE TEST 2
The Outsiders

I. Matching	II. Multiple Choice	III. Vocabulary
1. F	1. (A) (B) (C) ( )	1. Q
2. D	2. (A) (B) ( ) (D)	2. D
3. G	3. (A) (B) ( ) (D)	3. E
4. C	4. (A) ( ) (C) (D)	4. J
5. A	5. ( ) (B) (C) (D)	5. A
6. E	6. (A) (B) ( ) (D)	6. K
7. I	7. (A) ( ) (C) (D)	7. R
8. H	8. (A) ( ) (C) (D)	8. F
9. B	9. ( ) (B) (C) (D)	9. N
10. J	10. (A) (B) (C) ( )	10. H
		11. T
		12. L
		13. P
		14. C
		15. I
		16. B
		17. G
		18. O
		19. S
		20. M

UNIT RESOURCE MATERIALS

BULLETIN BOARD IDEAS - *The Outsiders*

1. Save one corner of the board for the best of students' writing assignments.

2. In conjunction with Lesson One, Activity 1, have students bring in one picture representing their heroes. (See Lesson One.) Use the time during Activity 1 for students to post their pictures on the board and explain what they represent.

3. Title the board THE OUTSIDERS. Post pictures of a blue Mustang, a water fountain, a church, and a vacant lot. Around the pictures, post quotes from the story.

4. Take one of the word search puzzles from the extra activities packet and with a marker copy it over in a large size on the bulletin board. Write the clue words to find to one side. Invite students prior to and after class to find the words and circle them on the bulletin board.

5. Post articles about gangs and their influences on their neighborhoods and society. Perhaps one of your local agencies will have information they would like to have posted . . . .

6. Do an anti-drug/anti-alcohol bulletin board: JUST SAY NO. There's a lot of good posters and information out there you can pick up for free.

7. Have students make posters and/or take photos (or have your newspaper or yearbook photographers take photos) of your students' Neighborhood Improvement Committees' work. Keep the photos and posters for use on your bulletin board for next year.

8. Title your board: BE AN INDIVIDUAL! Post pictures of people doing their own unique things--show them doing things different from "the crowd." Better yet, have students bring in pictures of themselves doing something they like to do & post those pictures on the board.

9. Make a bulletin board about THINGS TO DO illustrating things students can do besides hang out on the street corner (so-to-speak) after school and on weekends. Perhaps do a bulletin board about hobbies in conjunction with an extra activity about hobbies.

EXTRA ACTIVITIES

One of the difficulties in teaching a novel is that all students don't read at the same speed. One student who likes to read may take the book home and finish it in a day or two. Sometimes a few students finish the in-class assignments early. The problem, then, is finding suitable extra activities for students.

The best thing I've found is to keep a little library in the classroom. For this unit on *The Outsiders*, you might check out from the school library other related books and articles about gangs, heroes, being an individual, hobbies, neighborhoods, neighborhood groups or associations, safety tips for living in high crime areas, fire fighting, murder by accident, or information about good ways to "get out" of a bad situation.

Other things you may keep on hand are puzzles. We have made some relating directly to *The Outsiders* for you. Feel free to duplicate them.

Some students may like to draw. You might devise a contest or allow some extra-credit grade for students who draw characters or scenes from *The Outsiders*. Note, too, that if the students do not want to keep their drawings you may pick up some extra bulletin board materials this way. If you have a contest and you supply the prize (a CD or something like that perhaps), you could, possibly, make the drawing itself a non-refundable entry fee.

The pages which follow contain games, puzzles and worksheets. The keys, when appropriate, immediately follow the puzzle or worksheet. There are two main groups of activities: one group for the unit; that is, generally relating to the *Outsiders* text, and another group of activities related strictly to the *Outsiders* vocabulary.

Directions for these games, puzzles and worksheets are self-explanatory. The object here is to provide you with extra materials you may use in any way you choose.

1. If members of your class are involved in "gangs," have them openly discuss the reasons for their animosity towards other gangs. Ask if there are ways the sides can be reconciled. Compare and contrast gang activity in your area with the portrayal of gangs in the story.

2. Have a Peace Day on which members of your class (or school) try to get along together. If there is no gang activity in your area, you could take Peace Day to discuss conflicts in other areas and possible solutions to those conflicts.

3. Have students pair up with people they normally do not sit next to or closely associate with. Give the students 15 minutes to talk to each other to try to get to know each other better. If you want, you could rotate partners every 10 to 15 minutes for an entire class period.1. Pick a chapter or scene with a great deal of dialogue and have the students act it out on a stage. (Perhaps you could assign various scenes to different groups of students so more than one scene could be acted and more students could participate.)

4. Have students design a book cover (front and back and inside flaps) for *The Outsiders*.

5. Have students design a bulletin board (ready to be put up; not just sketched) for *The Outsiders*.

6. Have a "hobby day" when students can come in and show off their hobbies. You could also invite members of the community who have interesting hobbies to come in and share their hobbies with your class. That may give some students who don't have any hobbies some ideas that might interest them.

7. Have students choose one chapter of the story (with sufficient dialogue) to rewrite as a play. In conjunction with this assignment, have students write a composition explaining the difficulties they encountered in changing from one written form to another.

8. Look in your community for heroes--people who have done heroic things. Perhaps you have police, firemen, war veterans, or others who may have exciting stories to tell, or maybe your class would just like to have a little ceremony honoring the "heroes" of your community. That would be a good class project--to find and invite heroes (involving research and writing), and plan a class-period-long event to honor the heroes.

9. Show the film *West Side Story*. Compare and contrast it with *The Outsiders*.

WORD SEARCH - *The Outsiders*

All words in this list are associated with *The Outsiders*. The words are placed backwards, forward, diagonally, up and down. The included words are listed below the word search.

```
M Z H X F F D R G T W X N D X C Z M Z T K T K F
E P L M H R P O U O S T T F C M S B G S E B Q G
X K F B Z T O C O R O R B H R C O D E T B R O M
B R O T H E R S B L A D E M O U N T A I N L I F
K B B C L I A I T I B N R S T S T L H E D T U F
J B G B A L N S N B M A D S A E P K S E D N V E
W U U H L X F T P G Y U I Y R E E I N E R B N S
S O D A P O P Y O Y S D S A B E R K T N F U N V
D H D G S J R A O N E A G T L O O G O A G I D G
Y B C F E R O B U R E I X B A O T T V M L P N R
A I C R A M Y H S L C W M E B N S T W Y S E Q K
M X Q D U N C Q N Y J U S R T N G R L O M X L M
B K W M O H Z G T N R A R P I Z L W M E - Y D L
V N Q P J S C V D F Y R C W A M X W H L V B N W
G A L L A N T P R I D E E K L P G T H G I F I F
B A R B E C U E Q Y J H X H E P E J N S R N X T
F O U N T A I N W V N G Q K C T N R L T D V J T
```

ARM	DEAD	JACKET	RANDY
BARBECUE	DOUBLE	JOHNNY	RINGS
BLADE	FIGHT	JUDGE	RUMBLE
BLOOD	FIRE	KNIFE	SMOKE
BLUE	FOUNTAIN	LATE	SOCS
BOB	FROST	LOT	SODAPOP
BOOK	FUN	MARCIA	SPY
BOTTLE	GALLANT	MOTHER	TEXAS
BROTHERS	GOLDEN	MOUNTAIN	THEME
CHERRY	GOOD	MUSTANG	TIM
CHURCH	GREASERS	NEWSPAPER	TRAIN
CIGARETTES	GUN	OUTSIDERS	TURF
COKE	HAIRCUT	PAUL	TWO-BIT
DALLAS	HINTON	PONYBOY	WIND
DARRY	HOSPITAL	PRIDE	WINSTON

CROSSWORD CLUES - *The Outsiders*

ACROSS

1. What Johnny wanted Pony to stay
2. Gang symbol
4. The church caught on _____
6. Nightly _____
10. Another name for rumble
11. Police shot him
12. Condition of Bob, Dally and Johnny
13. Cherry threw hers into Dally's face
16. Place for printed accounts of news and editorials
19. She became a greaser spy
22. Johnny liked this land of southern gentlemen
25. Red body fluid
26. Dally pointed an unloaded one at the police
27. The west-end gang
28. Soda fought for this reason
29. _____ inhalation; firefighters get it
30. Hard-fighter Shepards first name
33. Johnny killed him
35. Place were Johnny died
38. Dally injured his getting Johnny out
40. Fight
42. Transportation to Windrixville
43. Johnny's murder weapon
44. He killed Bob and saved the children
45. Reason Darry fought; Pony's hair symbolized his

DOWN

1. Johnny's note said that there is still __ in the world
2. He acquitted Pony
3. Police were looking for Johnny and Pony toward __
4. Poet Robert
5. Tried to call off the big rumble
7. Johnny's gift to Pony; *Gone With the* __
8. Mustang color
9. Pony's eldest brother
10. Pony was almost drowned in it
13. Pony smoked them
14. Cherry is one for the greasers
15. Getting one upset Pony because he lost his trademark
17. *Gone With the* ____
18. Holden; he started a rumble
20. Author
21. Bob wore these on his fingers
23. Darry hit Pony because he was ___
24. Pony and Johnny fell asleep in the empty _____

25. Darry, Soda and Pony, for example
29. Middle brother
31. Cherry's Soc sidekick
32. East-end gang
33. Slang for knife
34. Kind of sandwiches Johnny ate
36. The narrator
37. Pony is assigned to write one
39. Johnny rejected his _____'s visit
41. Pony broke the end off one and threatened the Socs
42. Slang for area

	G	O	L	D	E	N		J	A	C	K	E	T			F	I	R	E
	O							U				E				R		A	
D	O	U	B	L	E			D				X		B	O		N		D
	D		O		F	I	G	H	T		D	A	L	L	A	S	D	E	A D
	O		O		O		E				S		U		T		Y		R
C	O	K	E		U			S				E							R
	I			H		N	E	W	S	P	A	P	E	R		C	H	E	R R Y
G	A	L	L	A	N	T		I		Y		A				I		I	
	A		A		I		A		N			U		L		N		N	
	R		T		R		I		D		B	L	O	O	D		T		G U N
	E		E		C		N				R				T		S	O	C S
	T			F	U	N				S	M	O	K	E			N		
	T	I	M		T			G		O		T					B	O	B
	E		A			R		D		H	O	S	P	I	T	A	L	A	R M
	S		R	U	M	B	L	E		A		E			O		H	A	O
			C			O		A		P		R			N		E	D	B T
T	R	A	I	N		T		S		O		S			Y		M	E	E H
U			A			T		E		P				B		E		C	E
F					L		R					O						U	R
F		K	N	I	F	E		S		J	O	H	N	N	Y		P	R I D E

___ 1. DALLAS   A. Police shot him

___ 2. GREASERS   B. Transportation to Windrixville

___ 3. TURF   C. Red body fluid

___ 4. CIGARETTES   D. Johnny's gift to Pony; *Gone With the Wind*

___ 5. GALLANT   E. The church caught on _____

___ 6. PAUL   F. Cherry threw hers into Dally's face

___ 7. BLOOD   G. Holden; he started a rumble

___ 8. COKE   H. Jay's _____

___ 9. MOUNTAIN   I. Johnny liked this land of southern gentlemen

___ 10. FIRE   J. *Gone With the* ___

___ 11. DOUBLE   K. Bob wore these on his fingers

___ 12. MUSTANG   L. Pony smoked them

___ 13. CHERRY   M. Johnny's murder weapon

___ 14. FUN   N. Blue Soc car

___ 15. KNIFE   O. Soda fought for this reason

___ 16. RINGS   P. Slang for area

___ 17. BOOK   Q. Dally injured his getting Johnny out

___ 18. TRAIN   R. Nightly _____

___ 19. WIND   S. East-end gang

___ 20. ARM   T. She became a Greaser spy

___ 1. BOOK

___ 2. KNIFE

___ 3. SPY

___ 4. GREASERS

___ 5. ARM

___ 6. GALLANT

___ 7. BLADE

___ 8. BOTTLE

___ 9. FOUNTAIN

___ 10. DEAD

___ 11. PONYBOY

___ 12. BARBECUE

___ 13. LOT

___ 14. SMOKE

___ 15. TURF

___ 16. CIGARETTES

___ 17. NEWSPAPER

___ 18. CHERRY

___ 19. RANDY

___ 20. FROST

A. _____ inhalation; firefighters get it

B. Pony and Johnny fell asleep in the empty _____

C. Place for printed accounts of news

D. Pony was almost drowned in it

E. Johnny liked this land of southern gentlemen

F. Kind of sandwiches Johnny ate

G. She became a Greaser spy

H. Pony smoked them

I. The narrator

J. Dally injured his getting Johnny out

K. East-end gang

L. Pony broke the end off one and threatened Socs

M. Johnny's murder weapon

N. Slang for area

O. Johnny's gift to Pony; *Gone With the Wind*

P. Cherry is one for the Greasers

Q. Tried to call off the big rumble

R. Slang for knife

S. Poet Robert

T. Condition of Bob, Dally and Johnny

KEY: MATCHING QUIZ/WORKSHEETS - *The Outsiders*

Worksheet 1	Worksheet 2
1. A	1. O
2. S	2. M
3. P	3. P
4. L	4. K
5. I	5. J
6. G	6. E
7. C	7. R
8. F	8. L
9. H	9. D
10. E	10. T
11. R	11. I
12. N	12. F
13. T	13. B
14. O	14. A
15. M	15. N
16. K	16. H
17. D	17. C
18. B	18. G
19. J	19. Q
20. Q	20. S

JUGGLE LETTER REVIEW GAME CLUE SHEET - *The Outsiders*

SCRAMBLED	WORD	CLUE
NGU	GUN	Dally pointed an unloaded one at the police
ATNIONFU	FOUNTAIN	Pony was almost drowned in it
ULAP	PAUL	Holden; he started a rumble
TROEHM	MOTHER	Johnny rejected his_____'s visit
SRRHETBO	BROTHERS	Darry, Soda and Pony, for example
NOTIHN	HINTON	Author
OPONYYB	PONYBOY	The narrator
LTAAGLN	GALLANT	Johnny liked this land of southern gentlemen
INSWONT	WINSTON	Dally's last name
IRSNG	RINGS	Bob wore these on his fingers
DRYAN	RANDY	Tried to call off big rumble
YRRAD	DARRY	Pony's eldest brother
HRYRCE	CHERRY	She became a Greaser spy
EBLDOU	DOUBLE	Nightly _____
ONJNYH	JOHNNY	He killed Bob and saved the children
OBKO	BOOK	Johnny's gift to Pony; *Gone With the Wind*
ITHGF	FIGHT	Another name for rumble
LBEAD	BLADE	Slang for knife
CUBERBAE	BARBECUE	Kind of sandwiches Johnny ate
REOTSSIUD	OUTSIDERS	The _____; book title
IMT	TIM	Hard-fighter Shepards first name
MAR	ARM	Dally injured his getting Johnny out
EBLU	BLUE	Mustang color
KTEAJC	JACKET	Gang symbol
PYS	SPY	Cherry is one for the Greasers
GEUDJ	JUDGE	He acquitted Pony
EDDA	DEAD	Condition of Bob, Dally and Johnny
TOSFR	FROST	Poet Robert
TLHSPOIA	HOSPITAL	Place where Johnny died
HCHCRU	CHURCH	Hide out that caught on fire
WNEPRSEAP	NEWSPAPER	Place for printed accounts of news and editorials
ATHUIRC	HAIRCUT	Getting one upset Pony because he lost his trademark
OBB	BOB	Johnny killed him
OTL	LOT	Pony and Johnny fell asleep in the empty ____
HEMET	THEME	Pony is assigned to write one
FIEKN	KNIFE	Johnny's murder weapon
OTLETB	BOTTLE	Pony broke the end off one and threatened Socs
SEARESGR	GREASERS	East-end gang
TMUSGAN	MUSTANG	Blue Soc car

VOCABULARY RESOURCE MATERIALS

VOCABULARY WORD SEARCH - *The Outsiders*

All words in this list are associated with *The Outsiders*. The words are placed backwards, forward, diagonally, up and down. The included words are listed below the word search.

```
V Z S G K Y Y L L U F E U R G K M K D F F C J G
Z I Z N C S N L H T B R X D X R K M C E Y D M J
P I T Y L D R E D L I W E B T N A N G I D N I M
G V N A L Q E E D E O C N L E E L S V N L U F Q
Y V T H L S S B R V N N Y O U W S S P E L W L J
F L E D A P U N A I A G E L N C I S L E E H O E
P G E L E L T O W T N I I D G C T L A E D R L C
R T D R I S A J U Z I N M S E N H A D R E M E T
L E A E A T F T Y T O N S L E T I A N E C R X D
S T C H T R E L I I P H G T E R A R L T R A Y D
E J G U X T T X T O G M N M U S G C O A L I S X
B A V F R P I C P Z N O E W A P S R I L N Y N M
M B S D U R I U H L C D R T C D O L O L P T J G
G N I R E V I U Q C O Q Q G N H R R Y G P M L B
L M B F N V N N P C W I K H E O J A G Q G M I Y
L A D O S L J B G P A N T Y L D C J S X F Y O G
V E C N A L B M E S E R B S L O U C H E D F Y C
```

ABRUPTLY	COWLICK	INDIGNANT	RESIGNEDLY
ACQUITTED	DEBATING	INHALATION	RESEMBLANCE
AGHAST	DENY	LEERY	RUEFULLY
AIMLESSLY	DESPERATE	LONED	SARCASM
ASSET	ELITE ....MADRAS		SLOUCHED
BEWILDERDLY	ELUDED	NONCHALANTLY	STUPOR
BEWILDERING	EXPLOITS	PITY	VEERED
COMPLICATED	GORGED	QUIVERING	VITAL
CONTEMPTUOUSLY	GRASPED	RARELY	WINCED
CONTENT	GROGGY	RECURRING	
CONVICTION	IMPLORINGLY	RELUCTANTLY	

VOCABULARY CROSSWORD CLUES - *The Outsiders*

ACROSS

2. Amazed, stupefied
5. Tuft of hair growing in a different direction
10. Cotton fabric shirt usually brightly colored
11. Suddenly
13. Swerved, turned aside from a course or direction
16. Strong belief
20. Not fully awake
22. Essential, necessary to life
24. Deciding
27. Disgusted, anger with contempt
28. Confusing; puzzling

DOWN

1. Wary, suspicious
3. Afraid, suspicious
4. Without direction, without purpose
5. Scornful, insolent
6, To shrink back as if from pain
7. Involved, complex
8. Worth
9. Trembling, shaking
11. Discharged completely, set free from a legal charge
12. Compassion for suffering
14. Satisfied, pleased
15. To declare untrue; contradict
17. Beseechingly
18. Selling alcohol where not legally available
19. Senses are deadened
21. Swallow with greediness
23. By oneself
25. A select body, the best
26. Understood

VOCABULARY CROSSWORD ANSWER KEY - *The Outsiders*

								L		A	G	H	A	S	T	A		
	C	O	W	L	I	C	K	E		A		P				I		
Q	O	I			O			E	S			P				M		
U	N	N		M	A	D	R	A	S	A	B	R	U	P	T	L	Y	
I	T	C		P		Y		E		C		E		I		E		
V	E	E	R	E	D	L		C		T	Q	H		T		S		
E	M	D				I		O			U	E		Y		S		
R	P	D	C	O	N	V	I	C	T	I	O	N				L		
I	T			E	A	T		M			T	S				Y		B
N	U			N	T	E	P				T	I		S				O
G	R	O	G	G	Y	E		N		L	E	V	I	T	A	L		O
	U		D		T	O				D	E	U	O			T		T
	S		R			R					P	N		L				L
	L		G	D	E	B	A	T	I	N	G	O		E		E		E
	Y		E		L			N		R		R		D				G
			D		I	N	D	I	G	N	A	N	T					G
					T			L		S								I
					E			Y		P								N
								B	E	W	I	L	D	E	R	I	N	G
								D										

122

VOCABULARY MATCHING WORKSHEET 1 - *The Outsiders*

___ 1. LEERY

A. To breathe into the lungs

___ 2. RARELY

B. Unbelieving

___ 3. INCREDULOUS

C. Imitating, ridiculing

___ 4. RESIGNEDLY

D. Deciding

___ 5. SARCASM

E. Likeness, similarity

___ 6. STUPOR

F. Uncommon, infrequent

___ 7. BEWILDERING

G. Without direction, without purpose

___ 8. PITY

H. Senses are deadened

___ 9. INHALATION

I. Driven to take any risk

___ 10. AIMLESSLY

J. Tuft of hair growing in a different direction

___ 11. MIMICKING

K. Cotton fabric shirt usually brightly colored

___ 12. DEBATING

L. Bitter cutting jest

___ 13. DESPERATE

M. Wary, suspicious

___ 14. COWLICK

N. Worth

___ 15. MADRAS

O. By oneself

___ 16. VITAL

P. Confused, perplexed

___ 17. LONED

Q. Compassion for suffering

___ 18. SOPHISTICATED

R. Giving up, accepting the future

___ 19. ASSET

S. Cultured, worldly

___ 20. RESEMBLANCE

T. Essential, necessary to life

VOCABULARY MATCHING WORKSHEET 2 - *The Outsiders*

___ 1. PITY

A. Essential, necessary to life

___ 2. AGHAST

B. Swallow with greediness

___ 3. BOOTLEGGING

C. Likeness, similarity

___ 4. RESEMBLANCE

D. Uncommon, infrequent

___ 5. RESIGNEDLY

E. Imitating, ridiculing

___ 6. ELITE

F. Indifferently

___ 7. INCREDULOUS

G. A select body, the best

___ 8. COMPLICATED

H. Confused, perplexed

___ 9. MIMICKING

I. Giving up, accepting the future

___ 10. BEWILDERING

J. Trembling, shaking

___ 11. EXPLOITS

K. Selling alcohol where not legally available

___ 12. ACQUITTED

L. Heroic acts, adventures

___ 13. RARELY

M. Compassion for suffering

___ 14. NONCHALANTLY

N. Involved, complex

___ 15. FLINCHING

O. Betraying fear, pain or surprise
   with an involuntary gesture

___ 16. GORGED

P. Gloomily, somber

___ 17. QUIVERING

Q. Unbelieving

___ 18. ELUDED

R. Amazed, stupefied

___ 19. SULLENLY

S. Escaped, avoided

___ 20. VITAL

T. Discharged completely, set free from
   a legal charge

KEY: VOCABULARY MATCHING WORKSHEETS - *The Outsiders*

Worksheet 1	Worksheet 2
1. M	1. M
2. F	2. R
3. B	3. K
4. R	4. C
5. L	5. I
6. H	6. G
7. P	7. Q
8. Q	8. N
9. A	9. E
10. G	10. H
11. C	11. L
12. D	12. T
13. I	13. D
14. J	14. F
15. K	15. O
16. T	16. B
17. O	17. J
18. S	18. S
19. N	19. P
20. E	20. A

VOCABULARY JUGGLE LETTER REVIEW GAME - *The Outsiders*

1. SGDREAP	1. GRASPED	Understood
2. PTDCSHSOEIIAT	2. SOPHISTICATED	Cultured; worldly
3. LTNOANAHII	3. INHALATION	To breathe into the lungs
4. TSESA	4. ASSET	Worth
5. NUSUDLECIRO	5. INCREDULOUS	Unbelieving
6. CEIDWN	6. WINCED	To shrink back as if from pain
7. UNVQGIEIR	7. QUIVERING	Trembling; shaking
8. OPINEORINMT	8. PREMONITION	Previous warning
9. DVREEE	9. VEERED	Swerved; turned aside
10. RGGDOE	10. GORGED	Swallowed with greediness
11. NICIFGHLN	11. FLINCHING	Betraying fear, pain or surprise with an involuntary gesture
12. TIADNNNIG	12. INDIGNANT	Disgusted; anger with contempt
13. AALNOTHNYLCN	13. NONCHALANTLY	Indifferently
14. YCNALTLRUET	14. RELUCTANTLY	Unwillingly
15. NTNOCTE	15. CONTENT	Satisfied; pleased
16. NLYSULEL	16. SULLENLY	Gloomily; somber
17. XIEPSOLT	17. EXPLOITS	Heroic acts; adventures
18. EDULSOHC	18. SLOUCHED	An ungainly gait
19. EDEDLU	19. ELUDED	Escaped; avoided
20. TIBOGGNLOGE	20. BOOTLEGGING	Selling alcohol where not legally available
21. RCIRURNGE	21. RECURRING	Returning; repeated
22. SRMADA	22. MADRAS	Brightly colored cotton shirt
23. ERYEL	23. LEERY	Wary; suspicious
24. ITYP	24. PITY	Compassion for suffering
25. ARRYEL	25. RARELY	Uncommon; infrequent
26. OLECDPAMCIT	26. COMPLICATED	Involved; complex
27. SDRNIYLEGE	27. RESIGNEDLY	Giving up; accepting the future
28. ICCWOKL	28. COWLICK	Tuft of hair growing in a different direction
29. TBDGIAEN	29. DEBATING	Deciding
30. SSLMLIYEA	30. AIMLESSLY	Without direction; without purpose